Super Cheap Alaska Travel Guide 2023

Redefining Super Cheap	11
How to Enjoy ALLOCATING Money in Alaska	24
How to feel RICH in Anchorage	27
Try an all-in-one accommodation	31
Get 50% off an Alaskan Cruise	32
State Park Lands	37
LOCAL INSIGHTS FOR DRIVING	39
More Itinerary Ideas	42
Priceline Hack to get a Luxury Hotel on the Cheap	48
Hotels with frequent last-minute booking discounts in Anchorage	49
Saving money on Alaska Food	54
How to be a green tourist in Alaska	56
How to use this book	60
OUR SUPER CHEAP TIPS…	61
How to Find Super Cheap Flights to Alaska	63
How to Find CHEAP FIRST-CLASS Flights to Alaska	67
More flight tricks and tips	71
How to Find CHEAP FIRST-CLASS Flights to Alaska	72
Visit Reindeer on the cheap	83
Get something for free	87

Explore Juneau	93
Mendenhall Glacier Visitor Center	95
Go Whale Watching	97
Go fishing	99
Visit Valdez	110
Go Gold Panning	111
Bush Mail Flight	113
Sitka National Historical Park	116
Whittier and Prince William Sound	118
Visit the Largest lake in Alaska	120
Breakdown	129
Money Mistakes in Alaska	133
The secret to saving HUGE amounts of money when travelling to Alaska is…	134
MAP of key attractions	137
RV Route MAP	138
Thank you for reading	141
Bonus Travel Hacks	143
Common pitfalls when it comes to allocating money to your desires while traveling	144
Hack your allocations for your Alaska Trip	147
MORE TIPS TO FIND CHEAP FLIGHTS	150
What Credit Card Gives The Best Air Miles?	156
Frequent Flyer Memberships	160

How to get 70% off a Cruise	161
Pack like a Pro	162
Relaxing at the Airport	165
How to spend money	166
How to save money while travelling	171
Travel Apps That'll Make Budget Travel Easier	172
How NOT to be ripped off	174
Small tweaks on the road add up to big differences in your bank balance	180
Where and How to Make Friends	183
When unpleasantries come your way…	184
Hacks for Families	194
Safety	197
How I got hooked on budget travelling	200
A final word…	202
Our Writers	203
Copyright	205

"The mountains are calling, and I must go." -John Muir

The Magical Power of Bargains

Have you ever felt the rush of getting a bargain? And then found good fortune just keeps following you?

Let me give you an example. In 2009, I graduated into the worst global recession for generations. One unemployed day, I saw a suit I knew I could get a job in. The suit was £250. Money I didn't have. Imagine my shock when the next day I saw the exact same suit (in my size) in the window of a second-hand shop (thrift store) for £18! I bought the suit and after three months of interviewing, without a single call back, within a week of owning that £18 suit, I was hired on a salary far above my expectations. That's the powerful psychological effect of getting an incredible deal. It builds a sense of excitement and happiness that literally creates miracles.

I have no doubt that Alaska's snow-capped mountains, crystal-clear lakes, and vast expanses of untouched wilderness will uplift and inspire you but when you add the bargains from this book to your vacation, not only will you save a ton of money; you are guaranteed to enjoy a truly magical trip to Alaska.

Who this book is for and why anyone can enjoy budget travel

Did you know you can fly on a private jet for $500? Yes, a fully private jet. Complete with flutes of champagne and reclinable creamy leather seats. Your average billionaire spends $20,000 on the exact same flight. You can get it for $500 when you book private jet empty leg flights. This is just one of thousands of ways you can travel luxuriously on a budget. You see there is a big difference between being cheap and frugal.

When our brain hears the word "budget" it hears deprivation, suffering, agony, even depression. But budget travel need not be synonymous with hostels and pack lunches. You can enjoy an incredible and luxurious trip to Alaska on a budget, just like you can enjoy a private jet flight for 10% of the normal cost when you know how.

Over 20 years of travel has taught me I could have a 20 cent experience that will stir my soul more than a $100 one. Of course, sometimes the reverse is true, my point is, spending money on travel is the best investment you can make but it doesn't have to be at levels set by hotels and attractions with massive ad spends and influencers who are paid small fortunes to get you to buy into something you could have for a fraction of the cost.

This book is for those who love bargains and want to have the cold hard budget busting facts to hand (which is why we've included so many one page charts, which you can use as a quick reference), but otherwise, the book provides plenty of tips to help you shape your own Alaska experience.

We have designed these travel guides to give you a unique planning tool to experience an unforgettable trip without spending the ascribed tourist budget.

This guide focuses on Alaska's unbelievable bargains. Of course, there is little value in traveling to Alaska and not experiencing everything it has to offer. Where possible, we've included super cheap workarounds or listed the experience in the Loved but Costly section.

When it comes to luxury budget travel, it's all about what you know. You can have all the feels without most of the bills. A few days spent planning can save you thousands. Luckily, we've done the planning for you, so you can distill the information in minutes not days, leaving you to focus on what matters: immersing yourself in the sights, sounds and smells of Alaska, meeting awesome new people and feeling relaxed and happy.

This book reads like a good friend has travelled the length and breadth of Alaska and brought you back incredible insider tips.

So, grab a cup of tea or coffee, put your feet up and relax; you're about to enter the world of enjoying Alaska on the Super Cheap. Oh, and don't forget a biscuit. You need energy to plan a trip of a lifetime on a budget.

GET A BARGAIN RIGHT NOW

Sign-up to our newsletter. They are never annoying because we ONLY EVER send links to our books when they are FREE.

supercheapinsiderguides.com

Super Cheap Alaska is not for travellers with the following needs:

1. You require a book with detailed offline travel maps. Super Cheap Insider Guides are best used with Google Maps - download before you travel to make the most of your time and money.
2. You would like thousands of accommodation, food and attraction recommendations; by definition, cheapest is often singular. We only include maximum value recommendations. We purposely leave out over-priced attractions when there is no workaround.
3. You would like detailed write-ups about hotels/Airbnbs/Restaurants. We are bargain hunters first and foremost. We dedicate our time to finding the best deals, not writing flowery language about their interiors. Plus, things change. If I had a pound for every time I'd read a Lonely Planet description only to find the place totally different, I would be a rich man. Always look at online reviews for the latest up-to-date information.

If you want to save A LOT of money while comfortably enjoying an unforgettable trip to Alaska, minus the marketing, hype, scams and tourist traps read on.

Redefining Super Cheap

The value you get out of Super Cheap Alaska is not based on what you paid for it; it's based on what you do with it. You can only do great things with it if you believe saving money is worth your time. Charging things to your credit card and thinking 'oh I'll pay it off when I get home' is something you won't be tempted to do if you change your beliefs now. Think about what you associate with the word cheap, because you make your beliefs and your beliefs make you.

I grew up thinking you had to spend more than you could afford to have a good time traveling. Now I've visited 190 countries, I know nothing is further from the truth. Before you embark upon reading our specific tips for Alaska think about your associations with the word cheap.

Here are the dictionary definitions of cheap:

- Costing very little; relatively low in price; inexpensive: a cheap dress.
- costing little labor or trouble: Words are cheap.
- charging low prices: a very cheap store.
- Of little account; of small value; mean; shoddy: Cheap conduct; cheap workmanship.
- Embarrassed; sheepish: He felt cheap about his mistake.
- Stingy; miserly:
  He's too cheap to buy his own brother a cup of coffee.

Three out of six definitions have extremely negative connotations. The 'super cheap' we're talking about in this book is not shoddy, embarrassed, or stingy.
We added the super to reinforce our message. Super's dictionary definition stands for 'a super quality'. Super Cheap stands for enjoying the best on the lowest budget. Question other people's definitions of cheap so you're not blinded to possibilities, poten-

tial, and prosperity. Here are some new associations to consider forging:

Shoddy

Cheap stuff doesn't last is an adage marketing companies have drilled into consumers. However, by asking vendors the right questions cheap doesn't mean something won't last. I had a $10 backpack last for 8 years and a $100 suitcase bust on the first journey.

A study out of San Francisco University found that people who spent money on experiences rather than things were happier. Memories last forever, not things, even expensive things. And as we will show you during this guide, you don't need to pay to create glorious memories.[1]

Embarrassed

I have friends who routinely pay more to vendors because they think their money is putting food on this person's table. Paradoxically, Cuban doctors are driving taxis because they earn more money; it's not always a good thing for the place you're visiting to pay more and can cause unwanted distortion in their culture - Airbnb pushing out renters is an obvious example. Think carefully about whether the extra money is helping people or incentivising greed.

Stingy

Cheap can be eco-friendly. Buying thrift clothes is cheap, but you also help the Earth. Many travellers are often disillusioned by the reality of traveling since the places on our bucket-lists are overcrowded. Cheap can take you away from the crowds. You can find balance and harmony being cheap. "Remember a journey is

---

[1] Paulina Pchelin & Ryan T. Howell (2014) The hidden cost of value-seeking: People do not accurately forecast the economic benefits of experiential purchases, The Journal of Positive Psychology, 9:4, 322-334, DOI: 10.1080/17439760.2014.898316

best measured in friends, rather than miles." – Tim Cahill. And making friends is free!

A recent survey by Credit Karma found 50% of Millennials and Gen Z get into debt traveling. **Please don't allow credit card debt to be an unwanted souvenir you take home.** As you will see from this book, there's so much you can enjoy in Alaska for free, some many unique bargains and so many ways to save money! You just need to want to!

Discover Alaska

Staggering mountains amidst glaciers clinging to their sides, soul-stirring wildlife, turquoise lakes, ancient glaciers, streams and rivers with countless salmon, towering icebergs, lively cities, a unique culture, historic mining communities and a thousand things in between. Alaska is as huge and diverse as it is beautiful. Home to 740,000 people, it covers 586 square miles. Alaska's scale is indescribably breathtaking. Indeed, the name "Alaska" comes from the word Alyeskadin meaning "big country" or "big earth" . In part, due to its sheer scale Alaska has the reputation of being among the most expensive destinations in the world. Fortunately, some of the best things in life are free (or almost free). This guides shows you how you can stretch your budget to enjoy a thrilling Alaskan experience minus the unwanted credit card bill.

History

Alaska became the fortieth state of the North American Union on 3 January 1959. Russia controlled Alaska until 1857, and due to the Russian influence there is still a large Eastern Orthodox Christian population with 49 parishes and 50,000 followers. The First Russian Orthodox Church was established in Kodiak in 1795.

Your Alaskan Experience

Visiting Alaska is a quite different experience depending on how you choose to navigate its huge land mass. if you travel by road to travel vs. taking a cruise. If you choose to go over land either by train or car/RV, keep your vehicle stocked with fruits and munchies because you never know how far the next rest stop will be.

You're not going to see all of Alaska unless you do a lot of flying, but you can see the best it has to over with a cruise and an RV or train trips. In the summer, trains go south to Seward and North to Denali Park. There's scant phone coverage and very few coffee shops to recharge your phone. Alaska is a place for 'doing' rather than observing.

Local people

The locals are known for their resilience, authenticity, helpfulness, and resourcefulness; when a moose is killed on Alaskan roads instead of the roadkill being discarded, highway troopers keep a running list of in-need families and deliver it to them. They (especially old-timers or "sourdoughs" as locals call them) love to talk about their near-death experiences. So if you're missing Netflix, just head to a bar to listen to a real thriller.

There are 231 federally recognized Indian tribes in Alaska. Most believe each living being has a spirit. The trees, plants, any "living" thing has a spirit. They respect the land, and in turn the land returns their respect.

During the spring, for instance, children are told not to disturb the river by throwing rocks, sticks or kicking the ice because it will disturb the Rivers peace. When the ice breaks up, they go down to the river to wash their faces. It is a form of cleansing their soul in hopes of not becoming ill throughout the next year.

Alaska's cities have a quaint quirky small-town feel. Alaskans love the outdoors but will not be polite to underprepared tourists so carefully check the packing list in this guide before you embark upon your Alaskan adventure.

Winter in the north
The south is warmer than the north, where there is endless darkness and bitter cold. The lowest temperatures ever recorded in Alaska: -79.8 degrees!

Summer in the south

Some of Alaska's Best Bargains

Public-Use Cabins

Public-Use Cabins are Alaska's best-kept secret. These 80 public-use cabins are located in the wilderness, with some easily reached from the road. Though they tend to be near remote lakes, streams, and saltwater beaches. The good news is, they cost just $20 a night. You MUST leave the cabin as you found it, restocking wood and amenities for the next group. They are bookable on a first-come, first-served reservation system. You can reserve up to six months in advance. The cabins located in State Parks must be booked through this website: https://www.alaska.org/public-use-cabins

Free flights

Fly to Alaska return for free when you spend more than $2,000 on an Alaskan Airlines credit card within the first 90 days. More details are here: https://www.alaskaair.com/content/credit-card/visa-signature

Do a free Gold-rush tour

Klondike Gold Rush National Historic Park Visitor Center in Skagway offers free walking tours focused on the Gold-rush at 9am, 10am, 11am, 2pm, and 3pm. More details here:
https://www.nps.gov/klgo/index.htm

Enjoy a Coffee for 25 cents!

When you visit Denali National Park, grab a coffee at nearby Eureka Lodge for just 25cents!

The next 10 pages contain psychological hacks for saving money in Alaska. If you are only interested in the tangible tips skip to How to Feel Rich in Alaska.

How to Enjoy ALLOCATING Money in Alaska

'Money's greatest intrinsic value—and this can't be overstated—is its ability to give you control over your time.' - Morgan Housel

Notice I have titled the chapter how to enjoy allocating money in Alaska. I'll use saving and allocating interchangeably in the book, but since most people associate saving to feel like a turtleneck, that's too tight, I've chosen to use wealth language. Rich people don't save. They allocate. What's the difference? Saving can feel like something you don't want or wish to do and allocating has your personal will attached to it.

And on that note, it would be helpful if you considered removing the following words and phrase from your vocabulary for planning and enjoying your Alaska trip:

- Wish
- Want
- Maybe someday

These words are part of poverty language. Language is a dominant source of creation. Use it to your advantage. You don't have to wish, want or say maybe someday to Alaska. You can enjoy the same things millionaires enjoy in Alaska without the huge spend.

'People don't like to be sold-but they love to buy.' - Jeffrey Gitomer.

Every good salesperson who understands the quote above places obstacles in the way of their clients' buying. Companies create waiting lists, restaurants pay people to queue outside in order to create demand. People reason if something is so in demand, it must be worth having but that's often just marketing. Take this sales maxim 'People don't like to be sold-but they love to buy and flip it on its head to allocate your money in Alaska on things YOU desire. You love to spend and hate to be sold. That means when something comes your way, it's not 'I can't afford it,' it's 'I don't want it' or maybe 'I don't want it right now'.

Saving money doesn't mean never buying a latte, never taking a taxi, never taking vacations (of course, you bought this book). Only you get to decide on how you spend and on what. Not an advice columnist who thinks you can buy a house if you never eat avocado toast again.

I love what Kate Northrup says about affording something: "If you really wanted it you would figure out a way to get it. If it were that VALUABLE to you, you would make it happen."

I believe if you master the art of allocating money to bargains, it can feel even better than spending it! Bold claim, I know. But here's the truth: Money gives you freedom and options. The more you keep in your account and or invested the more freedom and options you'll have. The principal reason you should save and allocate money is TO BE FREE! Remember, a trip's main purpose is relaxation, rest and enjoyment, aka to feel free.

When you talk to most people about saving money on vacation. They grimace. How awful they proclaim not to go wild on your vacation. If you can't get into a ton of debt enjoying your once-in-a-lifetime vacation, when can you?

When you spend money 'theres's a sudden rush of dopamine which vanishes once the transaction is complete. What happens in the brain when you save money? It increases feelings of security and peace. You don't need to stress life's uncertainties. And having a greater sense of peace can actually help you save more money.' Stressed out people make impulsive financial choices, calm people don't.'

The secret to enjoying saving money on vacation is very simple: never save money from a position of lack. Don't think 'I wish I could afford that'. Choose not to be marketed to. Choose not to consume at a price others set. Don't save money from the flawed premise you don't have enough. Don't waste your time living in the box that society has created, which says saving money on vacation means sacrifice. It doesn't.

Traveling to Alaska can be an expensive endeavor if you don't approach it with a plan, but you have this book which is packed with tips. The biggest other asset is your perspective.

How to feel RICH in Anchorage

You don't need millions in your bank to **feel rich**. Feeling rich feels different to every person. "Researchers have pooled data on the relationship between money and emotions from more than 1.6 million people across 162 countries and found that **wealthier people feel more positive "self-regard emotions" such as confidence, pride and determination.**"

Here are things to see, do and taste in Anchorage, that will have you overflowing with gratitude for your luxury trip to Alaska.

- While money can't buy happiness, it can buy cake and isn't that sort of the same thing? Jokes aside, Fire Island Rustic Bakeshop in Anchorage have turned cakes and pastries into edible art. Visit to taste the most delicious croissant in Anchorage.
- While you might not be staying in a penthouse, you can still enjoy the same views. Visit rooftop bars in Anchorage, like Williwaw Social to enjoy incredible sunset views for the price of just one drink. And if you want to continue enjoying libations, head over to Orso for a dirt-cheap happy hour, lots of reasonably priced (and delicious) cocktails and cheap delicious snacks.
- Walking out of a salon or barber shop with a fresh cut makes most people feel rich. As the maxim goes, if you look good, you feel good. If you crave that freshly blow-dried or trimmed look, become a hair model for Academy of Hair Design is a beauty and barber school in Anchorage. You'll receive a free or discounted cut/colour or wash. Of course, always agree on the look with your stylist.

Those are just some ideas for you to know that visiting Anchorage on a budget doesn't have to feel like sacrifice or constriction. Now let's get into the nuts and bolts of Anchorage on the super cheap.

Planning your trip

Do you need a passport?

U.S. citizens flying between another state and Alaska do not need a passport. However, those driving through Canada or traveling on a ferry or cruise ship with stops in Canada are required to carry one. All non U.S. citizens will need a passport and possibly other documents to enter.

When to visit

The first step in saving money on your Alaska trip is timing. **May is the best time to visit to save cash**. Most tours operate mid-May to mid-September, with the exception of those into Denali (mid-June to end of August). Peak season is mid-June to mid-August. Avoid this time - prices triple. By visiting in May you'll have 20-hour days to explore and save a huge chunk of cash on your RV, Airbnbs and tours. If you can't travel in May, mid to late September is also a great time to avoid tourist crowds and get reduced rates.

Be aware of the lack of time between sunset and sunrise. While the long sun-filled days sound enticing if you aren't used to the sun setting at 3am and rising at 6am it can be a strange adjustment especially for children. Make sure to pack an eye-mask for some much needed shut eye.
Its worth noting that summers in Alaska have been ridiculously hot the past few years, so be sure to stay hydrated and apply sunscreen frequently.

Don't despair if you are visiting during peak times there are innumerable hacks to save on accommodation in Alaska which we will go into detail on.

Combine a cruise and rent an RV

Doing a cruise along the Inside Passage and flying into Anchorage and driving around are two different experiences and landscapes. For the full Alaska experience - do both. We will discuss hacks for both to keep costs low.
If you're a group and want to travel the best value option is an RV. You can rent one for four people, which works out at $30 a night each. You can rent an RV through (like an Airbnb) for RV's for $120, which divided by two comes in at $60 per person plus gas but with the freedom of wheels you can explore so much more.
For families – especially those with younger kids or groups of 4 or 5 – renting a car or RV will SAVE YOU THOUSANDS. Just don't do it in winter or bad weather conditions, spring and summer driving in the south is beautiful, everything else will require chains on your wheels and a great deal of patience.

Rooms in Alaska

Hostels and hotels can cost upwards of $300 a night in some areas. Thankfully, you can find airbnbs or vrbo rentals for $30 a night. Rooms up fill fast. Book ahead to avoid paying A LOT more than you wanted if you don't want to book an RV. I recommend you take two weeks to experience Alaska. Try to see as much as you can via cruise and the Alaska Railroad (from Anchorage north to Fairbanks, and south to Seward or Whittier. Ride in the glass-domed upper cars and bring a good camera). If your budget is limited and you're not driving, base yourself in Seward where accommodation is cheapest.

Try an all-in-one accommodation

When you add up the cost of renting a car, kayaks, fishing gear, transporting of camping gear and accommodation it can cost a lot, especially if you are not a solo travel. If you're looking for a hassle-free way to experience Alaska take a look at Foster Alaska Cabins based in Kenai.

'EVERYTHING is included when you reserve a package with [Foster's Alaska Cabins](), besides your airfare to Anchorage and the cost of your fishing license. Packages are all-inclusive and come with: a rental vehicle, lodging, all meals and snacks, beer, wine, soda, water, guided trips and activities, live music, all of the necessary equipment and gear for the duration of your stay, and all fish processing and packaging.'

Prices start at $100 a night but the cost depends on the date, rate, number of guests. Contact them directly for a quote. https://fostersalaskacabins.com/

When you factor in a kayak rental for one person averages out at $79 per day all-in-one type accommodations can save you a lot of money!

Get 50% off an Alaskan Cruise

An average Alaska cruise can set you back $4,000. If you dream of cruising Alaska, but find the pricing too high, look at repositioning cruises. You can save as much as 70% by taking a cruise which takes the boat back to its home port.

These one-way itineraries take place during low cruise seasons (spring and fall in Alaska), when ships have to reposition themselves to locations where there's warmer weather.

To find a repositioning cruise go to vacationstogo.com/repositioning_cruises.cfm

Enter Anchorage (any port) or other ports you'd consider going from: Seattle, Juneau, Glacier Bay National Park, Haines, Sitka, Wrangell, and Thorne Bay all have repositioning cruises and book a cruise at half the normal cost.

If you don't find any deals on Vacations to Go check CruiseDirect and The Cruise Web.

Attention: Always check the number of days at sea and port calls. There's not much point taking the cruise if it only stops at two ports and neither interest you.

UPGRADE your cabin cheaply
If you're cruising to Alaska check to see if your cruise provider offers cabin upgrade bidding. You may be able to save 80% of the cost of a nicer cabin by booking the cheapest one and then bidding to upgrade. This works really well in low-season. Just bear in mind 'All bids are per person, based on double occupancy -- regardless of how many people are sharing the cabin. If you bid $200, you are committing to $400.'

Necessary Information for planning a trip to Alaska

- Cruises operate May to September

- The best time to see the Northern lights can be seen late August to March

- It's not dark 24/7 south of the Arctic Circle.

- You need a minimum of one week, but 2-3 weeks preferably.

- Hump back Whales arrive in Alaskan waters in April and leave in August

- There are polar bear tours in Kaktovik starting in early fall.

- There aren't any hikes in Alaska from May to September that won't have bear danger, but don't let it deter you. Most AlaskaN brown bears are active during early morning and dusk. If you make a lot of noise when hiking, wear bear bells, bring bear spray they will stay away.

Narrow your focus to save HUGE AMOUNTS OF MONEY

You don't have to cover huge distances to see Alaska at its best. Narrow the area you want to cover. Research and focus on the nature and wildlife you want to see and choose your dates carefully.

Tips on renting an RV

Renting a car or RV will give you the freedom to do what you want. The great thing about renting an RV is you can park anywhere that isn't private property. No need to pay to go to campgrounds every night.

Here are our tips for renting an RV:
1. The best RV prices are found in Anchorage
2. Rent direct from the owner of the RV with
2. 3. If you want to stay in campground check out https://www.alaska.org/where-to-stay/rv-parks-and-campgrounds to find the campground that'll suit your needs.
4. Rent with unlimited mileage due to the distances you will cover, you do not want to return the RV to a huge bill because you had to change route due to road blockages.
5. Rent using your credit card, most credit cards provide free in-surance for rented vehicles - but check with your provider before you rent.
6. Make sure your car rental company and insurer allows driving on the Dalton Highway if you do want to drive as a lot of companies prohibit driving on that road.

State Park Lands

Alaska is a place where RV travel can come with some rough outdoor living especially if you park in on any of the 3.3 million acres of state park lands.

Some basics to know:
Typical Cost: Free to $15
Water: Rarely
Electric: Rarely
Sewer: No
Most have a 15-night maximum stay

The following are the state parks with RV campsites and the amenities they have available:

- Chugach State Park - some with water hookups
- Big Delta State Historical Park - water hookups available
- Clearwater State Recreation Site
- Delta State Recreation Site
- Donnelly Creek State Recreation Site
- Quartz Lake State Recreation Area
- Birch Lake State Recreation Site
- Chena River State Recreation Site some with water and electric hookups
- Chena River State Recreation Area
- Harding Lake State Recreation Area
- Lower Chatanika River State Recreational Area - water hook-ups available
- Upper Chatanika River State Recreation Site - water hook-ups available
- Salcha River State Recreation Site
- Eagle Trail State Recreation Site
- Moon Lake State Recreation Site

- Tok River State Recreation Site

To find Free Campgrounds in Alaska, visit these sites:

https://ourroaminghearts.com/best-free-camping-sites-usa/
https://www.campendium.com/free-camping
https://www.freshoffthegrid.com/how-to-find-free-camping-usa-canada/
https://rvshare.com/blog/boondocking-in-alaska/

LOCAL INSIGHTS FOR DRIVING

1. Be aware of frost heaves, soft shoulders, and potholes. Potholes are most frequent after winter before they have been filled by the DoT.
2. If you need to pull over, make sure you do so on steady ground.
3. Don't spend so much time driving that you don't get to chill and relax and take in the beautiful landscapes and chat with locals.
4. Make sure to get a Milepost book. It mentions all mile markers on the highways in the state. Plus, some tell a story of the area or point out places you might not notice when driving by or highlight lakes to do some fishing and what fish they are stocked with. Fishing and cooking your own catch over the camper fire is a great way to keep costs down and truly enjoyable experience.
5. Due to weather some highways may not allow rental cars or RVs because of the roughness of the road. Always check on https://511.alaska.gov/ where you can and can't drive. The afflicted routes are usually: McCarthy road, Denali Highway, and Dalton Highway to Arctic Circle and beyond and the times driving may be prohibited tend to fall between October to March. If you're thinking of driving on dirt roads such as the McCarthy Road, make sure you have a full tank of gas and a full-sized tire for replacement.
6. Mind the tourists. When the cruise ships come in, people often toss their sense of self-preservation out of the window and will begin walking in the roads - so keep an eye out if you're driving there in the summer season.
7. Avoid leaving a trail of food which will lead curious animals' right to you.

8. Stock up on food and gas in larger towns. A few will even have a Walmart where you are able to spend the night for free. Larger cities with more resources mean that prices are lower since there is more competition.
9. Make sure you bring bug sprays, the mosquitos are no joke in Alaska especially when the ice melts.

Simple RV route

(all areas will be covered in detail further on)

1. Pick up the RV in Anchorage
2. Drive onwards to stop at Seward->Homer-> Talkeetna->De- nali->Fairbanks (see the Northern Lights! That's free and beyond incredible) ->Glennallen-
3. Drive back to Anchorage.

Highlights
Along the way you can enjoy free tours around Denali park, a glacier cruise out of Seward (the scenery along the fjords is like a wilder Norway) and a fishing trip in Homer.

More Itinerary Ideas

Seven Days

Day 1 - Arrive Anchorage in the evening. Take airbnb for one night. Most of the flights go through Seattle and arrive to Anchorage quite late.
Day 2 - Whittier.
pick up your RV, Start driving South visit Whittier.
On the way stop by Animal Conservation center.
In Whittier you can take jet ski or kayaks to see the Glacier closer. The road to Whittier is very picturesque, especially right before the tunnel and there are lots of waterfalls around.
Hikes to do in Whittier
- Portage Pass trail - small and nice hike (2-3 mile) to the lake and to see Glacier.
- Boat trip in Portage lake (to the Glacier)
Day 3 - Seward.
Go paddle boarding or kayaking between icebergs in Bear Glacier Bay. Bear bay is the best place to swim next to huge icebergs. Highly recommended to have a lunch afterwards in Le Barn Appetit Inn Creapery.
Day 4
Boat trip to the Kenai F'yords and ocean wild life.
Day 5-6 - Homer.
When traveling it's easy to fall into "doing" state of mind and constantly be hungry for the experiences. Slow down in the middle of your travel trip in Homer. Views to the bay, glaciers and green fields will help you find the present moment.
Day 7 - drive back to Anchorage along the way do either:
Reed Lakes Trail - our favorite hike. Quite challenging though.
Basin Lake trail - same place, easier than Reed Lakes, but still very beautiful.

Eight Days

Day 1: Take the train to Talkeetna ($90) Small hippy town with lots of character. Visit: Conscious Coffee, Nagley's General Store and Denali Brewing Company
Day 2: Denali 66 mile bus into Denali State Park to view Denali mountain (this is an 8 hour round trip so you see a ton!!), 49th State Brewing
Day 3: Denali Zip lining, hiking, midnight sun ATV ride
Day 4: Girdwood Crow Creek Mine, Lower Winner Creek Trail, Girdwood Brewing Company
Day 5: Girdwood / Whittier Hiked Byron Glacier, visit the Whittier Tunnel
Day 6-7: Seward Stayed at Orca Island Cabins, glamping style. From here you can kayak around Resurrection Bay.
Day 8: Anchorage - Visit the Anchorage Brewing Company. Fly home

7 Days (if you WANT to spend more money)

1. Land at Anchorage. Eat at Moose's Tooth (great restaurant highly recommended by many friends who live in Anchorage)
2. Drive around Hatcher Pass (you will see many beautiful places along that route, and it's about 1h away from anchorage).
3. Drive down to Homer and do halibut/salmon combo fishing Make sure to get your fishing license (currently due to Covid you must secure a fishing license online through the Alaska Department of Fish and Game. - http://www.adfg.alaska.gov/index.cfm?adfg=license.main). After a full day fishing trip, go to Salty Dawg (4380 Homer Spit Rd) for a drink.
4. On your next day in Homer hike the Kachemak State Park with glacier view. There are bears, so either bring spray or some kind of noise makers (Or you can pick up two rocks from the beach and made noises along the way by clicking the rocks).
5. Go to Kenai River, which is between Homer and Whittier and check out Alaska West Air for a fly out bear viewing/ river fishing combo trip on a seaplane. On a good weather day, you will get a glacier tour from the air. The view is amazing.
6. Drive up to Whittier and do glacier Jetski with Alaska Wild Guides.
7. On the way back to Anchorage, stop by Beluga point when is high tight to see if you can spot some beluga whales. They are there normally before sunset.

Hack your Alaska Accommodation

If you're not going to rent an RV, your two biggest expenses when travelling to Alaska are accommodation and food. This section is intended to help you cut these costs dramatically before and while you are in Alaska.

Hostels are the cheapest accommodation in Alaska but there are some creative workarounds to upgrade your stay on the cheap.

Use Time

There are two ways to use time. One is to book in advance. Three months will net you the best deal, especially if your visit coincides with an event. The other is to book on the day of your stay. This is a risky move, but if executed well, you can lay your head in a five-star hotel for a 2-star fee.

Before you travel to Alaska, check for big events using a simple google search 'What's on in Alaska', if you find no big events drawing travellers, risk showing up with no accommodation booked (If there are big events on, demand exceeds supply and you should avoid using this strategy). Start checking for discount rooms at 11 am using a private browser on booking.com.

Before I go into demand-based pricing, take a moment to think about your risk tolerance. By risk, I am not talking about personal safety. No amount of financial savings is worth risking that. What I am talking about is being inconvenienced. Do you deal well with last-minute changes? Can you roll with the punches or do you freak out if something changes? Everyone is different and knowing yourself is the best way to plan a great trip. If you are someone that

likes to have everything pre-planned using demand-based pricing to get cheap accommodation will not work for you. Skip this section and go to blind-booking.

Demand-based pricing

Be they an Airbnb host or hotel manager; no one wants empty rooms. Most will do anything to make some revenue because they still have the same costs to cover whether the room is occupied or not. That's why you will find many hotels drastically slashing room rates for same-day bookings.

How to book five-star hotels for a two-star price

You will not be able to find these discounts when the demand exceeds the supply. So if you're visiting during the peak season, or during an event which has drawn many travellers again don't try this.

On the day of your stay, visit booking.com (which offers better discounts than Kayak and agoda.com). Hotel Tonight individually checks for any last-minute bookings, but they take a big chunk of the action, so the better deals come from booking.com. The best results come from booking between 2 pm and 4 pm when the risk of losing any revenue with no occupancy is most pronounced, so algorithms supporting hotels slash prices. This is when you can find rates that are not within the "lowest publicly visible" rate. To avoid losing customers to other websites, or cheapening the image of their hotel most will only offer the super cheap rates during a two hour window from 2 pm to 4 pm. Two guests will pay 10x difference in price but it's absolutely vital to the hotel that neither knows it.

Takeaway: To get the lowest price book on the day of stay between 2 pm and 4 pm and extend your search radius to include further afield hotels with good transport connections.

Priceline Hack to get a Luxury Hotel on the Cheap

Priceline.com has been around since 1997 and is an incredible site for sourcing luxury Hotels on the cheap in Alaska. If you've tried everything else and that's failed, priceline will deliver.

Priceline have a database of the lowest price a hotel will accept for a particular time and date. That amount changes depending on two factors:

1. Demand: More demand high prices.
2. Likelihood of lost revenue: if the room is still available at 3pm the same-day prices will plummet.

Obviously they don't want you to know the lowest price as they make more commission the higher the price you pay.

They offer two good deals to entice you to book with them in Alaska. And the good news is neither require last-minute booking (though the price will decrease the closer to the date you book).

'Firstly, 'price-breakers'. You blind book from a choice of three highly rated hotels which they name. Pricebreakers, travelers are shown three similar, highly-rated hotels, listed under a single low price.' After you book they reveal the name of the hotel.

Secondly, the 'express deals'. These are the last minute deals. You'll be able to see the name of the hotel before you book.

To find the right luxury hotel for you at a cheap price you should plug in the
neighbourhoods you want to stay in, an acceptable rating (4 or 5 stars), and filter by the amenities you want.

You can also get an addition discount for your Alaska hotel by booking on their dedicated app.

Hotels with frequent last-minute booking discounts in Anchorage

Here are several four and five-star hotels that offer comfortable accommodations are centrally located, and frequently have heavy last-minute booking discounts:

1. The Lakefront Anchorage
2. Anchorage Marriott Downtown
3. Sheraton Anchorage Hotel & Spa
4. The Westin Anchorage
5. Hilton Anchorage
6. Crowne Plaza Anchorage-Midtown
7. Hyatt Place Anchorage-Midtown
8. Embassy Suites by Hilton Anchorage
9. Residence Inn by Marriott Anchorage Midtown
10. Home2 Suites by Hilton Anchorage/Midtown

How to trick travel Algorithms to get the lowest hotel price

Do not believe anyone who says changing your IP address to get cheaper hotels or flights does NOT work. If you don't believe us, download a Tor Network and search for flights and hotels to one destination using your current IP and then the tor network (a tor browser hides your IP address from algorithms. It is commonly used by hackers). You will receive different prices.

The price you see is a decision made by an algorithm that adjusts prices using data points such as past bookings, remaining capacity, average demand and the probability of selling the room or flight later at a higher price. If knows you've searched for the area before ip the prices high. To circumvent this, you can either use a different IP address from a cafe or airport or data from an international sim. I use a sim from Three, which provides free data in many countries around the world. When you search from a new IP address, most of the time, and particularly near booking you will get a lower price. Sometimes if your sim comes from a 'rich' country, say the UK or USA, you will see higher rates as the algorithm has learnt people from these countries pay more. The solution is to book from a local wifi connection - but a different one from the one you originally searched from.

How to get last-minute discounts on owner rented properties

In addition to Airbnb, you can also find owner rented rooms and apartments on www.vrbo.com or HomeAway or a host of others. Nearly all owners renting accommodation will happily give renters a "last-minute" discount to avoid the space sitting empty, not earning a dime.

Go to Airbnb or another platform and put in today's date. Once you've found something you like start the negotiating by asking for a 25% reduction. A sample message to an Airbnb host might read:

Dear HOST NAME,

I love your apartment. It looks perfect for me. Unfortunately, I'm on a very tight budget. I hope you won't be offended, but I wanted to ask if you would be amenable to offering me a 25% discount for tonight, tomorrow and the following day? I see that you aren't booked. I can assure you, I will leave your place exactly the way I found it. I will put bed linen in the washer and ensure everything is clean for the next guest. I would be delighted to bring you a bottle of wine to thank you for any discount that you could offer.

If this sounds okay, please send me a custom offer, and I will book straight away.

YOUR NAME.

In my experience, a polite, genuine message like this, that proposes reciprocity will be successful 80% of the time. Don't ask for more than 25% off, this person still has to pay the bills and will probably say no as your stay will cost them more in bills than they make. Plus starting higher, can offend the owner and do you want to stay somewhere, where you have offended the host?

In Practice

To use either of these methods, you must travel light. Less stuff means greater mobility, everything is faster and you don't have to check-in or store luggage. If you have a lot of luggage, you're going to have fewer of these opportunities to save on accommodation. Plus travelling light benefits the planet - you're buying, consuming, and transporting less stuff.

Blind-booking

If your risk tolerance does not allow for last-minute booking, you can use blind-booking. Many hotels not wanting to cheapen their brand with known low-prices, choose to operate a blind booking policy. This is where you book without knowing the name of the hotel you're going to stay in until you've made the payment. This is also sometimes used as a marketing strategy where the hotel is seeking to recover from past issues. I've stayed in plenty of blind book hotels. As long as you choose 4 or 5 star hotels, you will find them to be clean, comfortable and safe. priceline.com, Hot Rate® Hotels and Top Secret Hotels (operated by last-minute.com) offer the best deals.

Hotels.com Loyalty Program

This is currently the best hotel loyalty program with hotels in Alaska. The basic premise is you collect 10 nights and get 1 free. hotels.com price match, so if booking.com has a cheaper price you can get hotel.com, to match. If you intend to travel more than ten nights in a year, its a great choice to get the 11th free.

Don't let time use you.
Rigidity will cost you money. You pay the price you're willing to pay, not the amount it requires a hotel to deliver. Therefore if you're in town for a big event, saving money on accommodation is nearly impossible so in such cases book three months ahead.

What to do if you only find overpriced options
If when you're searching for accommodation, you can only find overpriced offers, it's likely that you're visiting at a time where demand outstrips supply. In this case, have a look at www.trustedhousesitters.com. You stay for free when you care for someones pets. If you really can't find a good deal, this can be worth doing but only you know if you want to make a commitment to care for someone else's pets while on vacation. Some find it relaxing, others don't. The properties in Alaska can be even more stunning than five-star hotels but if you're new to house sitting you might be against 10+ applicants, so make sure your profile is really strong before you apply for a sit. It could save you a small fortune and, who knows, you could even make some new (furry and non-furry) friends.

Saving money on Alaska Food

Food can take a significant bite out of your vacation budget. Save some money with these tips:

Eat like a local

Reindeer Sausage is a local speciality that won't break the bank. Reindeer meat is leaner and healthier than beef or pork and more sustainable.

Go Berry Picking

Far superior to their cultivated cousins Alaska berries are the best and picking them yourself in the great outdoors ups their value to 'priceless'. Look for tart crimson cranberries, plump bright blueberries, juicy raspberries and cloudberries. Here's where you can find them around Anchorage https://www.anchorage.net/blog/post/berry-picking-in-anchorage/

Fish and cook your own catch

With wild king salmon prices from $30 and $70 per pound, catching your own fish and cooking it over the campfire is a way to eat well and save a lot of money.

Eat at Food Trucks

You'll find an abundance of food trucks in Alaska. Here are the best ones in Anchorage:

Mochileros Street Food
A Guatemalan taco truck with bites from $5.

Preference is a Vegan food truck in east anchorage. Try the famous bowl for $13. You can split it between two people

Bennys Food Wagon is a Mexican Food truck with great lunch plates well worth the money and $1 sodas.

Breakfast or Lunch at bakeries

Bakery Outlet offers real low prices on a range of delicious baked goods.

Address: 105 E 56th Ave,

Franz Bakery Outlet is one of the Best discount bakeries in town.

Address: 2248 Spenard Rd

Visit supermarkets at discount times

Groceries are 26% more expensive in Alaska than mainland USA. The three main stores for grocery shopping in Anchorage are Walmart, Fred Meyer, and Safeway. Walmart is cheapest and the place you should stock up. You can find fresh produce discounted at 5pm. Food is more expensive in smaller towns because there's less competition so stock up in cities. There are also two Costco's in Anchorage offering great discounts on everything from bear spray to salmon.

How to be a green tourist in Alaska

Record breaking temperatures have resulted in thawing permafrost, thinning sea ice, and increasing wildfires.

It's important as responsible tourists that we help not hinder Alaska. There is a bizarre misconception that you have to spend money to travel in an eco-friendly way. This like, all marketing myths was concocted and hyped by companies seeking to make money off of you. In my experience, anything with eco in front of their names e.g Eco-tours will be triple the cost of the regular tour. Don't get me wrong sometimes its best to take these tours if you're visiting endangered areas, but normally such places have extensive legislation that everyone, including the eco and non-eco tour companies, are complying with. The vast majority of ways you can travel eco-friendly are free and even save you money.

Avoid Bottled Water - get a good water bottle and refill. The water in Alaska is safe to drink.
Bring a cotton tote with you when you venture out to shop.
Pack Light - this is one of the best ways to save money. If you find a 5-star hotel for tonight for $10, and you're at an Airbnb or hostel, you can easily pack and upgrade hassle-free. A light pack equals freedom and it means less to wash.
If you opt not to rent a car or RV, travel around Alaska on Bikes or e-Scooters or use Public Transportation.
Travel Overland - this isn't always viable especially if you only have limited time off work, but where possible avoid flying and if you have to compensate by off-setting or keeping the rest of your trip carbon-neutral by doing all of the above.

It goes without saying that if you're camping you must leave no trace.

Unique bargains we love in Alaska

Alaskan nature is boundless and free - and life-changing. Once you've been to Alaska, nature looks very different.

Here is a list of the best FREE nature adventures:
• Have you're breath taking away by the glaciers at Glacier Bay, Kenai Fjords, and Prince William Sound.
• Feel dumbfounded at the wide open tundra and rugged moun-tains at the Chugach mountains near Anchorange, Denali Park, or the Brooks Range.
• Explore Gold rush relics at Kennicott, Hope, and Independence Mine.
• Gaze at Bear, moose, caribou, dall sheep, and maybe even wolves at Denali (these animals are found all over the state, but Denali is the easiest place to see them)

- See Bald eagles just about anywhere in Southeast Alaska.
- Look out for Sea birds, seals and sea lions all along the coast.
- Hike around Homer. If you're bringing your four-legged friend, most hikes in Alaska are dog friendly except those with big boulders or glacial traverses.

How to use this book

Google and TripAdvisor are your on-the-go guides while traveling, a travel guide adds the most value during the planning phase, and if you're without Wi-Fi. Always download the google map for your destination - having an offline map will make using this guide much more comfortable. For ease of use, we've set the book out the way you travel, booking your flights, arriving, how to get around, then on to the money-saving tips. The tips we ordered according to when you need to know the tip to save money, so free tours and combination tickets feature first. We prioritized the rest of the tips by how much money you can save and then by how likely it was that you could find the tip with a google search. Meaning those we think you could find alone are nearer the bottom. I hope you find this layout useful. If you have any ideas about making Super Cheap Insider Guides easier to use, please email me philgattang@gmail.com

A quick note on How We Source Super Cheap Tips
We focus entirely on finding the best bargains. We give each of our collaborators $2,000 to hunt down never-before-seen deals. The type you either only know if you're local or by on the ground research. We spend zero on marketing and a little on designing an excellent cover. We do this yearly, which means we just keep finding more amazing ways for you to have the same experience for less.

Now let's get started with juicing the most pleasure from your trip to Alaska with the least possible money!

OUR SUPER CHEAP TIPS...

Packing List

The weather can change fast in Alaska so wear layers.

Shopping isn't cheap so we have prepared this list of must-haves.

Bring rain gear
It rains all year round. Bring rain proof outerwear. Waterproof pants, tops and hat are essential.

Packing List
- Rain boots
- Hiking boots
- Warm clothes
- Layers of Lycra - Wearing gym clothes under your normal clothes will keep you warm. Lycra is excellent at trapping heat.
- Warm pyjamas - fleece or similar
- Socks
- Ski Gloves
- Hat
- Scarf
- Sunglasses
- Headlamp
- DEET Mosquito spray. Mosquitoes are active in the peak summer months of June to August. When snow melts stagnant swamps are created allowing mosquitoes to breed.

- An Eye-mask for all travellers.

Wear your bulkiest items on the flight to avoid needing to check a bag, but if you need to check, make sure you do, its not cheap to buy things in Alaska.

INSIDER MONEY SAVING TIP
If you do need to buy some of these items in Alaska head to the second hand shop 'Second Run' in Anchorage for 90% off the normal sale price.

INSIDER CULTURAL INSIGHT
For every 100 women in Alaska there are 107 men...

How to Find Super Cheap Flights to Alaska

Luck is just an illusion. Anyone can find incredible flight deals. If you can be flexible you can save huge amounts of money. In fact, the biggest tip I can give you for finding incredible flight deals is simple: find a flexible job. Don't despair if you can't do that theres still a lot you can do.

Book your flight to Alaska on a Tuesday or Wednesday

Tuesdays and Wednesdays are the cheapest days of the week to fly. You can take a flight to Alaska on a Tuesday or Wednesday for less than half the price you'd pay on a Thursday Friday, Saturday, Sunday or Monday.

Start with Google Flights (but NEVER book through them)

I conduct upwards of 50 flight searches a day for readers. I use google flights first when looking for flights. I put specific departure but broad destination (e.g Europe) and usually find amazing deals.

The great thing about Google Flights is you can search by class. You can pick a specific destination and it will tell you which time is cheapest in which class. Or you can put in dates and you can see which area is cheapest to travel to.

But be aware Google flights does not show the cheapest prices among the flight search engines but it does offer several advantages

1. You can see the cheapest dates for the next 8 weeks. Other search engines will blackout over 70% of the prices.
2. You can put in multiple airports to fly from. Just use a common to separate in the from input.
3. If you're flexible on where you're going Google flights can show you the cheapest destinations.
4. You can set-up price tracking, where Google will email you when prices rise or decline.

Once you have established the cheapest dates to fly go over to skyscanner.net and put those dates in. You will find sky scanner offers the cheapest flights.

Get Alerts when Prices to Alaska are Lowest

Google also has a nice feature which allows you to set up an alert to email you when prices to your destination are at their lowest. So if you don't have fixed dates this feature can save you a fortune.

Baggage add-ons

It may be cheaper and more convenient to send your luggage separately with a service like sendmybag.com Often the luggage sending fee is cheaper than what the airlines charge to check baggage. Visit Lugless.com or luggage-free.com in addition to sendmybag.com for a quotation.

Loading times

Anyone who has attempted to find a cheap flight will know the pain of excruciating long loading times. If you encounter this issue use google flights to find the cheapest dates and then go to skyscanner.net for the lowest price.

Always try to book direct with the airline

Once you have found the cheapest flight go direct to the airlines booking page. This is advantageous in the current covid cancellation climate, because if you need to change your flights or arrange a refund, its much easier to do so, than via a third party booking agent.

That said, sometimes the third party bookers offer cheaper deals than the airline, so you need to make the decision based on how likely you think it is that disruption will impede you making those flights.

More flight tricks and tips

www.secretflying.com/usa-deals offers a range of deals from the USA and other countries. For example you can pick-up a round trip flight non-stop from from the east coast to johannesburg for $350 return on this site

Scott's cheap flights, you can select your home airport and get emails on deals but you pay for an annual subscription. A free workaround is to download Hopper and set search alerts for trips/price drops.

Premium service of Scott's cheap flights.
They sometime have discounted business and first class but in my experience they are few and far between.

JGOOT.com has 5 times as many choices as Scott's cheap flights.

kiwi.com allows you to be able to do radius searches so you can find cheaper flights to general areas.

Finding Error Fares

Travel Pirates (www.travelpirates.com) is a gold-mine for finding error deals. Subscribe to their newsletter. I recently found a reader an airfare from Montreal-Brazil for a $200 round trip (mistake fare!). Of course these error fares are always certain dates, but if you can be flexible you can save a lot of money.

Things you can do that might reduce the fare to Alaska:--
- Use a VPN (if the booker knows you booked one-way, the return fare will go up)
- Buy your ticket in a different currency

How to Find CHEAP FIRST-CLASS Flights to Alaska

Upgrade at the airport
Airlines are extremely reluctant to advertise price drops in first or business class tickets so the best way to secure them is actually at the airport when airlines have no choice but to decrease prices dramatically because otherwise they lose money. Ask about upgrading to business or first-class when you check-in. If you check-in online look around the airport for your airlines branded bidding system. For example KLM at Amsterdam have terminals where you can bid on upgrades.

Use Air-miles

When it comes to accruing air-miles for American citizens **Chase Sapphire Reserve card** ranks top. If you put everything on there and pay it off immediately you will end up getting free flights all the time, aside from taxes.

Get 2-3 chase cards with sign up bonuses, you'll have 200k points in no time and can book with points on multiple airlines when transferring your points to them.

Please note, this is only applicable to those living in the USA. In the Bonus Section we have detailed the best air-mile credit cards for those living in the UK, Canada, Germany, Austria, Spain and Australia.

How many miles does it take to fly first class?
First class from Bangkok to Chicago (one way) costs 180,000 miles.

Cheapest route from mainland USA

At the time of writing the cheapest way to get to Alaska is to fly from Seattle to Anchorage with Alaska Airlines. You can find one way tickets for $59, with returns from $120.

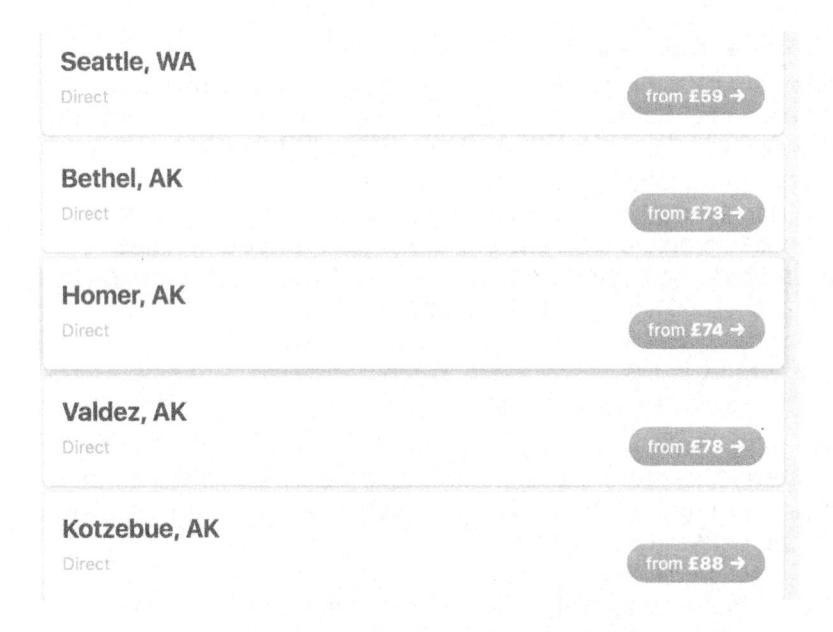

Seattle, WA
Direct — from £59 →

Bethel, AK
Direct — from £73 →

Homer, AK
Direct — from £74 →

Valdez, AK
Direct — from £78 →

Kotzebue, AK
Direct — from £88 →

If you're a US Citizen you can get a free flight to Alaska by getting an Alaskan Airlines credit card. When you spend $2k in first 90 days you get 40k miles. This equals a free flight and a $121 + taxes/fees companion fare. Just make sure you have the funds to pay the full balance off in full each month to avoid fees. Otherwise, the free flight can become very expensive.

Cheapest route from Europe

Dublin offers the cheapest flight to Anchorage. $600 return with Aer Lingus.

From	To	Depart	Return
Ireland (Any)	Anchorage Internation...	Cheapest mo...	Cheapest mo...

Direct flights only (none)

Estimated lowest prices only. Found in the last 15 days.

Select departure city

Dublin
1+ stops — from $599 >

Shannon
1+ stops — from $979 >

If you're flying to Alaska from somewhere else, please don't hesitate to e-mail me philgtang@gmail.com for free help finding a cheap flight.

The following pages will explain in detail how to find cheap fights.

Start with Google Flights

I conduct upwards of 50 flight searches a day for readers. I use google flights first. I put specific departure but broad destination (e.g Europe) and usually find amazing deals to the readers destination.

The great thing about Google Flights is you can search by class. You can pick a specific destination and it will tell you which time is cheapest in which class. Or you can put in dates and you can see which area is cheapest to travel to.

But be aware Google flights does not show the cheapest prices among the flight search engines but it does offer several advantages

1. You can see the cheapest dates for the next 8 weeks. Other search engines will blackout over 70% of the prices.
2. You can put in multiple airports to fly from. Just use a comma to separate your airports.
3. If you're flexible on where you're going Google flights can show you the cheapest destinations.
4. You can set-up price tracking, where Google will email you when prices rise or decline.

Once you have established the cheapest dates to fly go over to skyscanner.net and put those dates in. You will find sky scanner offers the cheapest flights.

Loading times

Anyone who has attempted to find a cheap flight will know the pain of excruciating long loading times. If you encounter this issue use google flights to find the cheapest dates and then go to skyscanner.net for the lowest price.

Always try to book direct with the airline

Once you have found the cheapest flight go direct to the airlines booking page. This is advantageous in the current COVID-19 cancellation climate, because if you need to change your flights or arrange a refund, its much easier to do so, than via a third party booking agent.

That said, sometimes the third party bookers offer cheaper deals than the airline, so you need to make the decision based on how likely you think it is that disruption will impede you making those flights.

More flight tricks and tips

www.secretflying.com/usa-deals offers a range of deals from the USA and other countries. For example you can pick-up a round trip flight non-stop from from the east coast to Johannesburg for $350 return on this site

Scott's cheap flights, you can select your home airport and get emails on deals but you pay for an annual subscription. A free workaround is to download Hopper and set search alerts for trips/price drops.

Premium service of Scott's cheap flights.
They sometime have discounted business and first class but in my experience they are few and far between.

JGOOT.com has 5 times as many choices as Scott's cheap flights.

kiwi.com allows you to do radius searches so you can find cheaper flights to general areas.

Finding Error Fares
Travel Pirates (www.travelpirates.com) is a gold-mine for finding error deals. Subscribe to their newsletter. I recently found a reader an airfare from Montreal-Brazil for a $200 round trip (mistake fare!). Of course these error fares are always certain dates, but if you can be flexible you can save a lot of money.

Things you can do that might reduce the fare to Alaska:--
- Use a VPN (if the booker knows you booked one-way, the return fare will go up)
- Buy your ticket in a different currency

How to Find CHEAP FIRST-CLASS Flights to Alaska

Upgrade at the airport

Airlines are extremely reluctant to advertise price drops in first or business class tickets so the best way to secure them is actually at the airport when airlines have no choice but to decrease prices dramatically because otherwise they lose money. Ask about upgrading to business or first-class when you check-in. If you check-in online look around the airport for your airlines branded bidding system.

Use Air-miles

When it comes to accruing air-miles for American citizens **Chase Sapphire Reserve card** ranks top. If you put everything on there and pay it off immediately you will end up getting free flights all the time, aside from taxes.

Get 2-3 chase cards with sign up bonuses, you'll have 200k points in no time and can book with points on multiple airlines when transferring your points to them.

Please note, this is only applicable to those living in the USA. In the Bonus Section we have detailed the best air-mile credit cards for those living in the UK, Canada, Germany, Austria, Spain and Australia.

Award Hacker

If you're planning on using points to buy a First or Business Class flights check AwardHacker.com to find the best route to redeem your points.

How many miles does it take to fly first class?
To give you an idea of the points it will require to fly first-class to Alaska. First class from Bangkok to Chicago (one way) costs 180,000 miles. Award Hacker will give you accurate predictions.

Getting Around Alaska

Going anywhere in Alaska requires lots of driving. People's homes, schools, offices are spread out. Driving in the winter is risky with the ice and lack of daylight. Driving in the summer months is a much more pleasurable experience. If you can't or don't want to drive there are a couple of other options to get around:

Trains: expensive in Alaska but the best way to get around the country on a budget and see the scenic routes. Views from the train are scary and exciting.

Bus: small shuttles connect most of Alaska's interior highways to Canada. Bus schedules can be found here: https://www.alaska.org/advice/alaska-bus-schedules

Air: The only way to get to some places but very expensive.

Drive - there's an app called 'share' which allows you to rent a car from $0.19 per minute + more for the Kilometre's but it's cheaper than a car rental and you can do hourly, daily or even weekly packages. You just scan the QR code on the code, hop in and drive.

A quick overview of Alaskan cities/towns

'**Alaska** is divided administratively into 19 organized boroughs and one Unorganized Borough (which is divided into 10 non-administrative census areas) and contains 149 incorporated cities. Here are the best ones to visit:

Anchorage: The largest city in the state. Great place to Anchor yourself (pun intended) if you're on a budget. You can take the train from here easily, which is the cheapest way to get around if you don't rent an RV.

Seward: Seward is a seaside town which boasts a fabulous sea life centre, amazing cruises, picture perfect hikes, kayaking, dogsled tours, whale watching cruises, fishing charters, hiking, and great views.

Juneau: Juneau became the capital in 1906. At the time Anchorage didn't exist and Fairbanks was a remote settlement but Juneau had a thriving mining industry and was only a short trip away from Seattle. Alaska's capital is located in the Southeast. Explore Alaska's panhandle, Mendenhall Glacier and nearby Glacier Bay National Park. The best budget experience is to hike up mount Roberts trail and then buy a $5 souvenir to ride the tram down for free. The original Alaska brewery is out in lemon creek and Juneau is home to more great breweries with lots of beer tours and tastings available.

Homer: A long strip of land with shops, art galleries, seafood restaurants and waters offering the best halibut and salmon fishing.

Talkeetna is the Denali gateway town. Its tiny but has a quaint and quirky feel, on a clear day, you can see Denali. The town is filled with cute shops, cool restaurants, a brewery, lots of different tours (if you're willing to pay for them, They can be pricey.). The best free experience is to picnic by the river. Park your RV on the banks of the Susitna River at mile marker 104 (just over the north side of the bridge) on the Parks Highway. Also pay a visit to the National park office, where mountaineers go before summiting Denali. They offer a free advice and a video about climbing Denali.

Fairbanks: Visit Fairbanks to experience Alaska's fierce interior and to see the Northern Lights.

Skagway: set along the popular cruise route the Inside Passage. It's home to gold-rush-era buildings, now preserved as part of the Klondike Gold Rush National Historical Park. Red Onion Saloon in Skagway offers a brothel tour. A Madam will take you through the streets and tell you story of the gold rush and how the brothel played a role. Matanuska Valley: Just 35 miles north of Anchorage. The Mat-Su Valley is actually two Valleys - the Matanuska Valley and the Susitna Valley, thus, Mat-Su.

Whittier: A sleepy town on the west side of Prince William Sound is remote. Most of the residents live in a single 14-story building called Begich Towers. Go for coastal mountain glaciers and tidewater scenery.

Valdez: Thompson Pass outside of Valdez has some of the best ski touring in all of Alaska.

Barrow (Utqiagvik):The annual whale harvest and celebration is an amazing sight to behold.

Nome:. Not reachable by road. Plane only

Bethel: Not reachable by road. Plane only

Kotzebue: very remote and no road access to other parts of the state.

INSIDER HISTORICAL INSIGHT
After the atrocities of Kristallnacht in Europe where Jews were killed and many of their businesses destroyed, the then USA Secretary of the Interior Harold L.
Ickes proposed that Jews resettled in Alaska, creating a Jewish state. Understandably the idea was not favoured by fleeing Jewish refugees...

Do The Cheapest Cruise

Price wise you cannot beat The Alaska State Ferry System also known as The Alaska Marine Highway. Their small cruise ships may be somewhat Spartan compared to the expensive cruises, but they take the same route through Alaska's Inside Passage and if you book ahead, you can even take your car or camper. Also, having shallower draught, they get much closer to land and glaciers and provide a much more better experience. . The cruise is good and ccces n Alaska than the ports you stop at on the cruise. Make sure you consider renting a car or an RV to truly experience Alaska.

State Ferry Map

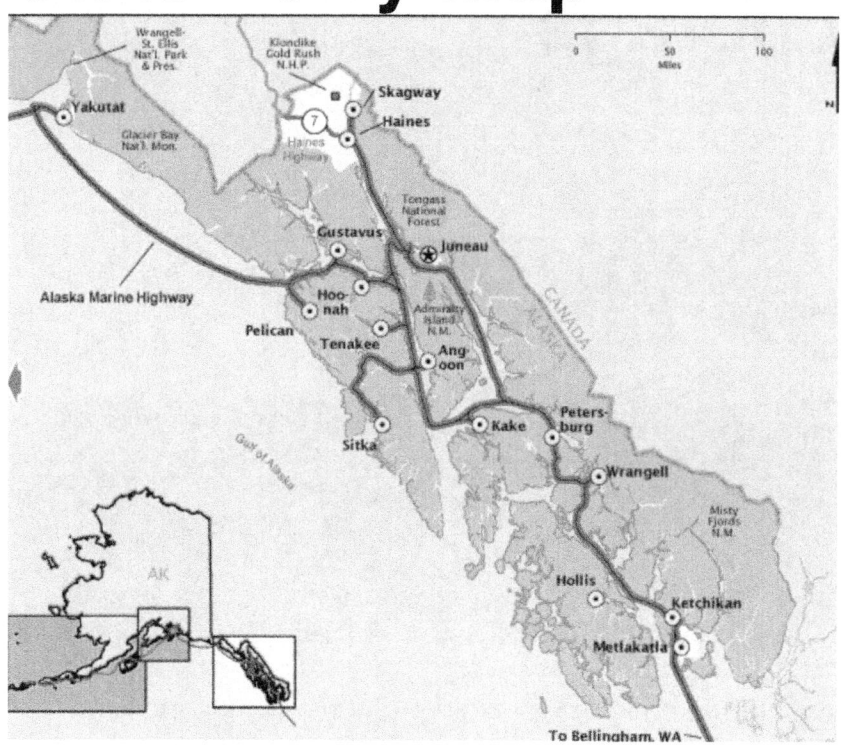

See The best of Anchorage

Anchorage offers breathtaking wilderness, history, and unique culture. It's a great introduction to Alaska and a great jumping off point with a rental car or RV. You'll no doubt spend a few nights in Anchorage, if just for the airport as most flights arrive late.

Anchorage feels like any big city, so if you're looking for more of an outdoor experience, stay down the road in Alyeska. Its about 30mins south of Anchorage, a tiny little mountain town and its ski runs are the best in state.

If you want to explore anchorage stay downtown for one or two days. Alyeska is on the way to Seward, if you're driving from Anchorage you could always stop along the way.

There's a lot to see without leaving Anchorage. You can take a hike up flattop, go to any of the thousands of creeks and parks. The buses are mediocre but will get you from A to B and there is Uber and Lyft. Anchorage offers Unparalleled Wildlife. Point Woronzof Road is the starting point for those keen to see Moose, bald eagles, bears, mountain goats, sheep, beluga whales, porcupines, rabbits, marmots, ravens, otters and wolves.

INSIDER MONEY SAVING TIP

There's an abundance of cheap things to do in Anchorage. Here are the best:

1. Rent a bike with TourSaver and bike the coastal trail
2. Go hiking in the Chugach Mountains
3. Go fishing at Ship Creek with a free rented rod (details below).
4. Splurge $5 to visit Alaska Botanical Garden to learn about Alaska's unique Forna and flora. You can also take a guided tour through the Botanical Gardens for just $15. Learn more here: https://www.airbnb.com/experiences/104132

INSIDER MONEY SAVING TIP

Many Alaska Department of Fish and Game (ADF&G) offices have fishing rods to lend for **FREE**. Find full details and your closest office here: https://www.adfg.alaska.gov/index.cfm?adfg=FishingSportFishAK.rodloaner

Visit Reindeer on the cheap

The Sant Claus Village is some 386 miles from Anchorage. If you don't want to spend six hours driving you can visit Williams Reindeer Farm. Located just outside of Anchorage you can feed and learn about reindeer first hand for $15 entry per adult and $13 children (3-11). Book your visit here: https://www.reindeerfarm.com/

INSIDER INSIGHT
Did you know carrots are not part of Reindeer's everyday diet? Reindeer actually struggle to chew them without top front teeth. Also, males typically lose their antlers in November whereas female reindeer keep theirs much longer. Meaning Santa Claus' reindeer may have been all female, since they are depicted with horns on Christmas Eve.

The Top free things to experience around Anchorage

• Powerline pass in anchorage is nice if you've got snow shoes or ice cleats. The drive up has a beautiful view of the city just very steep.
• Eagle River Nature Center is an Amazing park, the park ranger is very friendly and they have different trails depending how long you want to be there.
• Matanuska glacier is about two hours from anchorage. At 27 miles long by 4 miles wide, it is the largest glacier accessible by car in the United States.

INSIDER INSIGHT
If you travel to Anchorage in the winter, there is a greater opportunity to see the northern lights. Beware in the summer, the sun hardly ever sets.

Anchorage Map

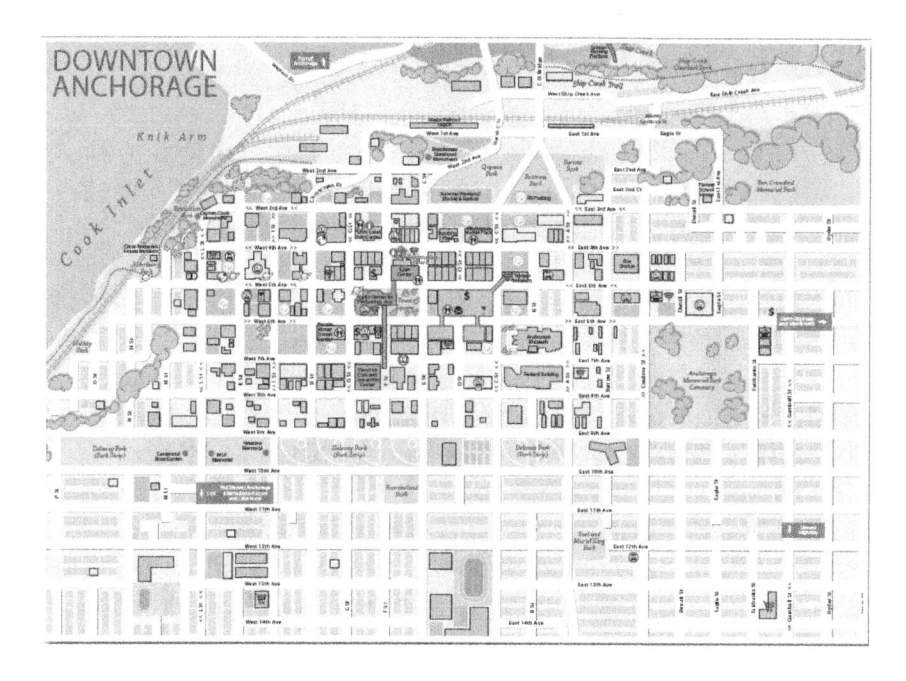

Get around Anchorage for FREE

Google for free Lyft credit and open a new account. You can get up to $50 free credit, which could cover your transport for your whole time in Anchorage.

Anchorage's top two attractions

The Alaska Native Heritage Center and the Anchorage Museum are best enjoyed with the Culture Pass Joint Ticket for $29.95. You'll get free entry to both and free shuttle transportation between them. Plus by visiting them rather than flying to Kotzebueyou are saving $500 on airfare and still learning about native culture.

Visit the Mountain View neighborhood to sample Anchorage's diversity in its its ethnic grocery stores.

Over 90 languages are spoken in the city's schools and, in 2010, Anchorage's Mountain View neighborhood was found to be the most diverse census tract in the US. After Native Alaskans, Asians/Pacific Islanders make up the bulk of the neighborhood's diversity. You can cycle the Ship Creek Bike Trail to its end in Mountain View.

Nightlife
If you don't go out you'll miss out on some great venues – the clubs and bars make it hard to catch some sleep in Anchorage. Go to Chilkoot Charlies on your first night in Anchorage. The live band is phenomenal. The Hard Rock Cafe in Anchorage puts on free comedy every First Fridays of each month, they feature a new line-up of Alaska's best stand-up comedians. Go to the 2nd floor of Hard Rock Cafe for free laughs.
Bear Tooth theatre pub offers classic Alaskan warmth and is a great place for drinks.

Get something for free

It's not news that the pandemic disrupted supply chains and contributed to major delays in shipping causing prices to increase. Researchers at at the University of Pennsylvania's Wharton School found that the average American family had to spend roughly $3,500 more in 2021 than in 2020 for the same goods and services due to inflation. One great way to save money in Alaska is to peruse local Freecycle, Trashnothing and Free in Alaska Facebook sites. If you find you need to buy something, whether that be a charger or torch in Alaska check these sites before. You can often find incredible freebies here that will cost you only the time to pick them up. Here is a list of the best free stuff websites in Alaska:

https://www.facebook.com/marketplace/anchorage/free/

https://anchorage.craigslist.org/search/zip

https://trashnothing.com/beta/anchorage-freecycle

Easy day trips from Anchorage

Portage Glacier is only an hour drive south of Anchorage. You can rent kayaks in Anchorage, take the ferry out to the glacier from the visitors center, or you can hike from Whittier. You could take the train there. And visit nearby Spencer Glacier,(only accessible by train), and kayak next to the glacier there.

Girdwood is a cute, small town 45 mins south of Anchorage. There you'll find lots of good easy hikes: Winner Creek Trail and the Byron Glacier Trail are the best.

Explore Denali Park

Denali National Park is the highlight of land tours available to cruise passengers. This mountain's name, which means 'high one,' is derived from Athabascan language. Denali was formed millions of years ago during an uplift of the Earth's crust. It is the third-tallest mountain in the Seven Summits (the highest mountains on each continent). The mountain has two distinct summits, the North Summit is higher and the South Summit is lower.

Denali is home to 169 species of birds, most of which are migratory. Other animals include wolves, marmots, caribou, and bears. In addition to these animals, visitors can also view amphibians, including wood frogs. These creatures hibernate in the winter and can be found in the park during springtime.

The upper half of Denali is permanently covered with snow and has five massive glaciers, with the longest glacier covering 71 kilometers (44 miles) long. The cold that prevails on Denali is extreme: temperatures can drop below -75 degrees Fahrenheit and wind chills can reach -118 degrees Fahrenheit. At this height, it can be dangerous to attempt to climb Denali.

Free shuttle buses serve the entrance area, which encompasses the Railroad Depot, Park Headquarters and several miles of trails. The park is huge and you can only drive so far into the park (and it's not far) before you need to take the paid shuttle. You need to book the shuttle ahead of time and pay for it. Booking details are here: https://www.nps.gov/dena/planyourvisit/shuttles.htm

INSIDER MONEY SAVING TIPS

You can park 10 miles south of the park entrance at one of the many pull offs on the highway for FREE, and then park in the park for day hikes and tours. You can only drive the first 15 miles of the 92 mile Park Road (not to be confused with Park Highway).

To go further you have to take a bus. Don't take the Tundra Wilderness Tour if you want to go into the park, there is a cheaper green shuttle bus that goes just as far for about half the price. It's not 'guided' but does the same thing. There's also a yummy and cheap ice cream shop at the mercantile at the park entrance and a laundry area if you need to clean some clothes.

There are free ranger led tours and a dog kennel show. You don't have to sign up in advance. The up-to-date schedule is here: https://www.nps.gov/dena/planyourvisit/calendar.htm

if you're driving an RV there make sure you stock up on groceries before you go; the more touristic a place you're going to, the more expensive the groceries.

INSIDER INSIGHT

If you're stuck for somewhere to park you're RV near Denali, Visit Healy, 14 miles from Denali National Park. It is literally in the middle of no where. There are great places all over to park and camp and some really beautiful views.

Listen to and watch GLACIERS calve

One of the most amazing sights in Alaska is watching and hearing tidewater glaciers 'calve' icebergs (the releasing of small to massive chunks of glacier into the water). Active tidewater glaciers can be viewed from tour boats in Glacier Bay National Park, Kenai Fjords National Park or Prince William Sound.

There are some 100,000 glaciers in Alaska, Alaska is one of the few places in the world where active glaciation occurs. Glacier ice absorbs all the colors of the spectrum except blue, which is why they often look blue.

The largest glacier in Alaska is the Malaspina, which sits at the base of Mt St Elias and blankets 850sq miles.

The cheapest way to see Glaciers is from the state ferry. Watch out for sea lions and horned puffins too.

Explore Juneau

Known for its incredible wildlife — both on land and by sea Juneau is one of the most popular cruise ports in Alaska. You can reach Juneau by the state's ferry system, the Alaska Marine Highway, in summer and winter. You can't drive all the way to Juneau without taking the ferry due to the extremely rugged terrain surrounding the city.

The best way to see Juneau is on The Mt Roberts Tramway. It costs $25 and you can ride as many times you want. The tram travels 1800 ft from street level to top of the mountain which offers some great views of the valley. The bar and dinning area on top are reasonably priced.

The hikes in Juneau are all incredible, but one of the most unexplored is the Rainforest Trail which has a little beach halfway through the walk.

After the hiking indulge in the tastiest and freshest fish taco you'll find in Alaska at Deckhand Dave's Fish Tacos a food truck that's permanently parked in the Franklin Food & Brew Court.

Mendenhall Glacier Visitor Center

Only 13 miles from downtown Juneau is the Mendenhall Glacier Visitor Center. The visitor center building is an interesting building all by itself with views of the glacier as it recedes from sight and the falls which were not visible before the center was built. It's only $5 per person to visit and includes free ranger tours. The are an abundance of nearby trails, which are all groomed but none go all the way to the glacier. East Glacier Trail is where you can catch a glimpse of a black bear

To get there if you're not driving: half-hourly Capital Transit bus is cheaper ($2), but drops you 1.5 miles short of the Mendenhall visitor center.

Kayaking

You can venture within a safe distance of the massive, awe-inspiring face of the glacier under a **limited kayaking USFS** permit. Here is a link to one of the cheaper tours: https://www.viator.com/tours/Juneau/Mendenhall-Glacier-View-Sea-Kayaking/d941-5474P30

If you like kayaking, kayak the rivers and not the bays in Alaska, you see much more. The top places for kayaking are:

- Moose River - great if you don't want to kayak a ton, stay in the big parts.
- Russian River to Skilak Lake is amazing. The best trails are along Skilak Lake Rd.
- Yukon River: Eagle to Circle.
- Tanana River: Fairbanks to Nenana

Be sure you are protected because rivers are very popular bear spots.

Go Whale Watching

Juneau is arguably the best whale watching spot in Alaska. The nutrient-rich waters around Juneau are whale feeding grounds. Whether you're visiting Juneau independently on a cruise, it's worth getting out on the water for a few hours to see these magnificent creatures.

The whale-watching in nearby Stephens Passage is so good that some tour operators offer to refund your money if you don't see at least one whale.

The best time to whale watch is from April to November, when approximately 600 humpbacks inhabit the waters of the northern Inside Passage.

Whale watching tours are offered in Juneau and near Glacier Bay. The boats depart from Auke Bay, and most tours last three to four hours. Prices average out at $140.https://www.viator.com/Juneau-tours/Dolphin-and-Whale-Watching

If you don't want to spend money on a whale watching tour go to The Chatham Straits or Cooks Inlet. Here you'll find some of the best whale viewing spots. You can go there via RV and watch from shore. Three hours is normally enough to spot a hump back from May to August but of course the best and most reliable whale watching really requires going out in a boat.

Go fishing

The Copper River is home to three species of salmon: King, Sockeye, and Coho. The King salmon, (also known as Chinook) is the largest salmon in the world and has an average weight of 45 pounds. It has a rich red flavor and firm texture. Sockeye salmon is the second fattiest salmon with similar firm texture and red color. Coho has an excellent mild salmon flavor and a reddish-orange meat that flakes well when cooked.

All three can be caught from the pure and pristine waters of Copper River in both lakes and rivers. From May through September, Copper River King, Sockeye, and Coho salmon return to the river.

'For first-timers Salmon Grove campground on the Klutina River is the perfect for catching some of the best salmon in Alaska. Avid and beginner fisherman alike will enjoy bank-fishing for Copper River red salmon right from the campground. It is easily waded and crossed. Guests can spread out and fish every inch of the river.'

Fishing licenses are required in order to fish in Alaska. You need to apply online: https://www.adfg.alaska.gov/Store/ Prices vary on age and residency.

There are thousands of streams in Alaska full of Rainbows, Graylings and Dollys. There's nothing better than a fish caught cooked on an open campfire in the company of great people and surrounded by trees and water. And it will only cost you the cost of the licence. As mentioned above you can often get fishing gear for free from the Alaska Department of Fish and Game.

Marvel at the Aurora Borealis

The northern lights are present due to lower levels of light pollution and the clear, crisp air. September, October, March and April are some of the best months to view the Northern Lights, also called the aurora borealis. The lights are known to be brighter and more active for up to two days after sunspot activity is at its highest. Several agencies, such as NASA and the National Oceanic and Atmospheric Administration, monitor solar activity and issue Aurora alerts when they are expected to put on a particularly impressive show, so check there websites. https://www.nasa.gov/

Fairbanks is the best place to see them. If you're not driving an RV, stay at Billie's Backpackers Hostel. It is the cheapest and best quality place we found near the lights. Get up at 1:30 am - to be rewarded with the best light show.

To see the Northern Lights you must have 3 things aligned:
1. It has to be dark enough. By late August there will be enough darkness to see them.

2. Solar flares cause them, so there must be solar flares going on.
3. No clouds. This website predicts the Aurora Borealis appearances: https://www.aurorahunter.com/northern-lights-forecast.html

Visit Fairbanks

Fairbanks was a gold town so you'll find historic gold mining related museum's like the Alaska Mining Hall of Fame. You'll also find Santa's house, Reindeer, the auto museum and access to the Artic circle. Almost 10,000 students attend The University of Alaska Fairbank so there's lots of partying options and cheap eats.

Chena Hot Springs is a must-visit in Fairbanks. Taking a dip in the hot springs when the outside temperature is negative is the best feeling. The best value option is to take a day pass to the pool so that you can experience the hot springs during both day and night times when the Northern Lights may appear. A single admission is $15.00 and the day-pass is $25. Knowledgeable Staff offer free Green house and geothermal tours.

Don't miss the Aurora Ice Museum at Chena Hot Springs. Here you can view ice sculptures from two world champion ice carvers Steve and Heather Brice included in the Chena Hot Springs price admission.

Keep in mind when booking a tour that the road to get to Aurora Ice Museum is icy but drivable. Give yourself extra time to get there.

If you don't want to see the Northern Lights from the hot springs, Murphy's dome in Fairbanks is absolutely amazing for star gazing. It's a little bit of a trek from Fairbanks, but worth it.

The University of Alaska Fairbanks is home to LARS (large animal research station) where you can see musk oxen and caribou. They offer private tours for groups for up to 40 from $200. You can email them to see if you can join another group: https://www.uaf.edu/lars/outreach/tours.php

If you are feeling adventurous you can drive or take a day trip to the Arctic Circle (189 miles north of Fairbanks). If you drive be sure you have enough food for the journey and that you are insured to drive on the Dalton Highway.

Cruise Seward

Seward is only 2.5 hours south of Anchorage. If you drive there, stop at Turnagain Arm (great views) and Girdwood along the way for gold panning and hiking.

The sea life centre is a must-visit in Seward. Here marine mammals are rehabilitated and you can learn all about Alaska's diverse marine life. Alaskan residents get free entrance on Wednesdays to sea life centre. The entrance for non-Alaskan residents is $29.95. Kids under two go free. The good news is, For a closer look at marine life, you can take a kayak trip to Resurrection Bay from Seward. Expect to see porpoises, otters, eagles, and harbor seals. The Tosina Beach route is best.

Kenai Fjords boat trips are very popular from Seward. The ride can be bumpy. The crew point out wildlife and when you get close to the glaciers you can practically reach them from deck.

The cheapest options for boat tours are the half-day tours, which cost about half the price of full-day tours. Prices start at $69.

Even though it's only 12 miles from Seward, Fox Island in Resurrection Bay feels blissfully remote. You can only get here by boat—on trips offered in Kenai. It will truly make you fall in love with coastal Alaska, plus you'll see many whales, orcas, and puffins but this is the pricer cruise and only full day options are available as they normally include the Kenai Fjords.

A cheaper activity in Seward is to take the Shuttle to Exit Glacier and do a hike up to the glacier. It's easy, safe and just $10 for a round trip.

Watch Bears fish salmon

The Brooks Camp

Located in Katmai National Park, Brooks Camp is the best place on earth to see brown bears and many like the one above will be eagerly fishing for salmon. The Brooks Camp Campground costs $12 per person per night or you can park for free nearby in a secluded area. If you want to park there you need a reservation: https://www.nps.gov/katm/planyourvisit/brooks-camp.htm

Interestingly, Anan Creek (near Juneau) is the only place here where brown and black bears live side-by-side.

Hike the Chilkoot Trail

Follow in the footsteps of the Gold Rush. The Chilkoot was used from 1897 to 1899 by thousands of prospectors to reach the Klondike and Upper Yukon Valley during the Klondike gold rush.

It's a great hike for almost any level of hiker. Just remember to have all the proper RAIN GEAR and supplies. Take your time and enjoy the views. Take full advantage of info and suggestion of park rangers. And Remember to pack snacks.

Go Snorkelling in Ketchikan

Think it's crazy to go snorkeling in Alaska? With a wetsuit and proper gear, it is a fantastic and memorable experience. You get to see barnacles feeding, along with urchins, sea stars, and sea cucumbers. This is an ocean lover's must-do adventure. You can find tours from $80.

If you do go to Ketchikan, Deer Mountain has lots of inspiring hiking trails. Rainbird trail is one of the best. If you're looking for more nature walks, Settlers' Cove, has very easy flat trails walking in the woods and a peaceful beach. You can also find many wild berries growing around

Interesting to know: Ketchikan is famous for commercial salmon fishing and Haida and Tlingit heritage. The largest collection of Native American totem poles in the world is found in Ketchikan.

In Ketchikan there's also a free downtown loop bus you can take to see the city. You literally can't miss it - it has spawning salmon painted all over it. It's open from May through September. Board on Water Street, Berth 4.

Visit Valdez

Valdez's town motto is: "Valdez, Alaska... because even Mother Nature has favorites"

Undeniably Valdez is a spectacular mix of tidewater glaciers, forests and mountains unequaled in the State.

During normal summers the population of 3,500 almost TRIPLES due to tourism. You can reach Valdez by The Alaska Marine Highway Ferry.

Worthington Glacier and Keystone Canyon are the two FREE must-sees. You can reach the Keystone Canyon through one of the many trails alongside it.

Go Gold Panning

Crow Creek Gold Mine

On your way back to Anchorage stop at Girdwood, about an hour from Anchorage and go gold mining at Crow Creek Mine. Established in 1896 you'll find dozens of adorable old fashioned houses, complete with antique furniture and furnishings. It's a great activity for kids and most visitors find flakes of gold.

$24 adult, $15 ages 12 & under | 9am - 6pm Daily, Mondays (Jun - Aug) 9am - 9pm

Escape the crowds

Alaska Tourist attractions will take a wrecking ball to your bank balance. They are popular for a reason you might say, but there are many incredible things to see, people to meet and food to try in Alaska without big ticket entry prices or lines. If you are easily overwhelmed by crowds visit the obvious attractions as early as possible, peak people flow is 11 am to 3 pm so get up early to enjoy the attractions serenely. Alaska being the huge land mass it is, has plenty of hidden gems that aren't commercialised or crowded. Here are the best:

- Eklutna Lake in Anchorage.

- Glacier Gardens Rainforest Adventure in Juneau.

- Pyrah's Pioneer Peak Farm in Palmer.

- Petroglyph Beach in Wrangell.

- Anan Bear and Wildlife Observatory in Wrangell.

Not super cheap but worth the money

Bush Mail Flight

The best money you can spend in Alaska is on delivering mail with a pilot in rural Alaska. You can accompany a pilot to visit 12 small villages as part of his mail delivery route. If you do the cheapest cruise - The Alaska Marine Highway use the money saved to pay for this. Its $199 - and guaranteed the best money you will spend in Alaska. Here is more information: https://www.warbelows.com/bush-mail-flights

Fish in Homer

Even by Alaskan standards, Homer is stunning. Its a 4-5 hour drive south of Anchorage depending on weather. This hippie-ish town is one of the best places in Alaska for Halibut and Salmon fishing. It's unfortunately not super cheap; the best-value chartered fishing tour is with O'-Fish'ial Charters of Alaska. Alongside the fishing you can expect to see see glaciers calving in the fjord, sea-lions, otters, Puffins and humpback Whales, but its not cheap. Prices start at $200 a day per person.

If you're going to Homer purely for sightseeing check out the free art Galleries on Pioneer Avenue and make sure you enjoy the best hike in Homer: The Homestead Trail at Rogers Loop Road. Here's a run-down of the best things to do in Homer.

1. Check out the homer spit, it's got cute shopping and great places to eat but pricey. When the tide pulls back at night you can find hundreds of starfish there. Its quite breathtaking.

2. Take Makos water taxi over to do the Grewingk Glacier hike (it's on your own, no cellphone signal, ask when the water taxi will pick you up before you leave)

3. Eat sweet treats at Two Sisters Bakery. The lemon tart and homemade lemonade are the bakeries best.

4. Take horseback riding classes at Rocking J ranch from $40. https://rockingjranch-ak.com/what-we-offer.

KODIAK ISLAND

You can take the ferry with your car to Kodiak Island; Alaska's largest fishing port, famous for catches of king crab and salmon. The ferry ride takes nine-and-a-half hours costing $37 per person each way. They have sleeping cabins that range from about $80-$130.

Sitka National Historical Park

Sitka is the oldest federally park in Alaska. President Benjamin Harrison designated it as park in 1890.

Sitka is the 6th largest seafood port by value in the US. Salmon, Trout, Char, Grayling, Halibut, Rockfish, and Lingcod are abundant in the waters here so it makes for a great base for anglers.

Unfortunately its not on the road system and is only accessible by air or water making it a costly experience.

Alaska Airlines offers daily flights from Anchorage, Fairbanks, Juneau, Ketchikan, and Seattle to Sitka or you can skip the $500 return airfare and cruise there in the summer

The park has Lots of history. The rangers are very helpful and knowledgeable about the areas history and the people. And The park has many authentic Tlingit and Haida totem poles as well as an exhibit on how they were made.

The Russian Bishop's House, once the Russian Mission Orphanage, is a historic house museum is a very good source of history and displays. Free tours of the upper floor in the Bishop's House are operated at fixed times. You can find an up-to-date schedule here: https://www.nps.gov/sitk/learn/historyculture/russian-bishops-house.htm

Whittier and Prince William Sound

60 miles south of Anchorage is the beautiful and peculiar city of Whittier. I say peculiar because most of the residents live in a single 14-story building called Beich Towers.

As the gateway to Prince William Sound there's stunning natural beauty and its the only town that has a one-way tunnel into it.

You can go on a Custom boat tour of Prince William Sound from Whittier, do a Glacier Jetski adventure, Take a Day Cruise, rent a kayak or visit the Prince William Sound Museum.

Arguably, Prince William Sound is the best place in Alaska to see spectacular coastal scenery and tidewater glaciers calving into the ocean.

Prince William Sound is also where wildlife reach some of their greatest numbers in Alaska. Resident marine mammals include humpback, sei, fin, minke, and killer whales as well as Steller sea lions, harbor seals, and sea otters and furbearers, sheep, and goats also abound. Though rugged and wild, the sound is easy to access.

Thes 70-mile-wide gulf is dotted with islands that reach from west from the Gulf of Alaska to the Kenai Peninsula.

You can Cruise, kayak, or jet ski in the Sound to see impressive tidewater glaciers and a huge array of animals. The best price performance tour goes from Whittier. It's costly at $195 but you'll get up close with the glaciers and get to see a range of marine wildlife.

More information is here: https://www.viator.com/tours/Anchorage/Phillips-Cruises-26-Glacier-Tour-Self-Drive-from-Anchorage

INSIDER TIP
If you catch some fish in Whittier, Whittier Fees Custom Seafoods Can help store your fishes in their freezer for a reasonable price and help you pack up so you can bring them with you back home.

Visit the Largest lake in Alaska

There are three million lakes in Alaska. They are larger than the water systems of Massachusetts and Vermont combined. Many of these lakes are in valleys carved by glaciers, and can be very deep. In fact, one of the largest lakes in Alaska, Lake Clark, is over a thousand feet deep.

Iliamna Lake is located in southwest Alaska, about 100 miles west of Seldovia. The lake shares its name with the nearby community of Iliamna and the Iliamna River. It is the largest lake in Alaska, covering over a million acres. It is also the largest freshwater lake in the state.

The largest lake in Alaska, Lake Iliamna is 30 miles across and nearly 100 miles long. It has excellent fishing opportunities for salmon and trout. It also provides some of the best wildlife viewing in Alaska. Visitors can visit the lake by boat, and fishing lodges also offer lodging, food, and tour opportunities. Many fishermen have heard of the legendary Iliamna Lake Monster.

Lake Iliamna is about the size of Connecticut. It is surrounded by a National Park. The lake is also home to the only wild white sheep in the world, the Dall Sheep. The lake is a great place to go for a relaxing day trip, and if you have time, take a cruise. The largest lake in Alaska, Lake Iliamna is 30 miles across and nearly 100 miles long. It has excellent fishing opportunities for salmon and trout. It also provides some of the best wildlife viewing in Alaska. Visitors can visit the lake by boat, and fishing lodges also offer lodging, food, and tour opportunities. Many fishermen have heard of the legendary Iliamna Lake Monster.

Lake Iliamna was named after a native tribe in 1802. Local myths have a large blackfish living in the lake. Local residents have also heard tales of a lake monster, similar to the Loch Ness Monster. Despite the fact that this monster is not a real animal, many people believe that it exists and is dangerous. The Anchorage Daily News has even offered a $100,000 reward for clear evidence of its existence.

It takes approximately 2 hours by plane to get from Anchorage to Iliamna Lake and tickets start at $190.

Shows or Films made in, or about Alaska

These shows and films will help you get a better understanding of where you're going without having to move from your sofa. It's worth noting, the government put a ton of money into benefitting those that filmed in Alaska, which are in turn bringing tourists to the region.

Into The Wild
This biographical film about the story of Christopher McCandless, a young man wanders into the wilds of Denali National Park to avoid the material world, he ends up dying in an abandoned bus. Note: People who talk about Into The Wild are really annoying to locals.

The Grey
Liam Nelson doing his thing in the wilds of Alaska.

Insomnia
Psychological thriller is set in the fictional fishing town of Nightmute, Alaska. Al Pacino works a murder investigation.

Mystery, Alaska
Alaska is chosen to host a hockey game against the New York Rangers of the National Hockey League after an article appears about their weekly Saturday night games in Sports Illustrated the townspeople get a little… overexcited.

Big Miracle (2012)
This nature drama based on actual events. A couple fighting to save a family of gray whales trapped in the icy waters of the Arctic Circle.

Need to Know before you go

Currency: US Dollar

Language: English and Yupik, a Native American language.

Money: Widely available in the towns.

Visas: Check http://www.doyouneedvisa.com/

Mobile Data:
AT&T have the best network coverage in Alaska. You can pick up a sim at most stores. Walmart is cheapest.

Time: GMT - 9

When to Go
High Season: June - July
Shoulder: May - September (cheapest months)Low Season: September to May - expect rain

Important Numbers
911

Getting Out of Alaska Cheaply

Plane

At the time of writing Alaska Airlines are offering the cheapest flights onwards. Take advantage of discounts and specials. Sign up for e-newsletters from local carriers including Alaska Airlines to learn about special fares. Be careful with cheap airlines, most will allow hand-luggage only, and some charge for anything that is not a backpack. Check their websites before booking if you need to take luggage.

Anchorage has cheap onward flights to the USA (Seattle), Mexico, Canada, Costa Rica and Iceland.

From	To	Depart	Return
Anchorage Internatio...	Everywhere	Cheapest m...	(One Way)

Direct flights only

Estimated lowest prices only. Found in the last 15 days.

United States	from £43
Mexico	from £159
Canada	from £169
Costa Rica	from £178
Iceland	from £212
Puerto Rico	from £242

Airport Lounges

You don't need to be flying business or first class to enjoy an airport lounge. Here are three methods you can use to access lounges at Alaska airport:

- Get or use a credit card that gives free lounge access. NerdWallet has a good write-up about cards that offer free lounge access. www.nerdwallet.com/best/credit-cards/airport-lounge-access

- Buy onetime access. They start at $23 and often include free showers and free drinks and food.

- Find free access with the LoungeBuddy app. You pay an annual fee of $25 to use the app.

Avoid these tourist traps or scams

Alaska is relatively new to tourism so there isn't the developed scams as you see in other places. It's worth noting that there is a known gang problem in Anchorage - with most of the crime centred on drugs. Spenard and Mountain View are two areas tourists should avoid in Anchorage. Follow these tips to stay ahead of the scammers:

- Use common sense, don't walk at night alone.

- Use Uber or Lyft - some taxi's will try to overcharge.

- Book accommodation ahead of time - prices skyrocket in summer months

- Get ready to haggle if you rent an RV.

- Beware of changing weather conditions and the need for chains on wheels. Travelling through Alaska requires careful planning.

RECAP: How to have a $5,000 trip to Alaska on a $1,000 budget

Find a cheap flight
Using the strategy we outlined you can snag a ticket to Alaska from the states from $60 return. Potential saving $1,000.

Combine Cruise and rent a shared Rv
The easiest way to see Alaska is to cruise up the Inside Passage. Combine that with renting an RV (the best campground in Alaska is the Starrigavan Recreation Area which has stunning costal scenery.) and Alaska will leave a lasting impression on your heart and mind but not your bank balance. Potential saving $2,000.

Book a repositioning cruise
Cruises go to towns and villages only accessible by air or land, so you if you want to see more of Alaska's remote regions, a repositioning cruise offers the best value. Potential saving: $500 on each airfare to remote places.

Book Airbnbs ahead of your visit
Accommodation fill up fast in Alaska so make sure you book airbnbs before your trip, if you're planning to stay in some. Hotels can run $300 so stick to Airbnbs! Potential saving $800.

Cook your own food
The Alaskan salmon and halibut are widely eaten, but the Alaskan King Crab is most famous. You can buy these delicious delicacies relatively inexpensively at supermarkets to cook in your RV or Airbnb. Restaurants are very expensive due to the short tourist season and the high labour costs. In Anchorage stock up at Fred Meyer's and Walmart, both are huge, offer fair prices and have no sales tax. Potential saving $500.

Get free fishing rod rentals
The Alaska Department of Fish and Game Loan Anglers Fishing Gear Free of Charge!

Go to museums/ attractions on the cheap.
Get cultured for free, or for cheap by using combi tickets and coupon books. Potential saving $1,000.

Do all the free stuff first
The natural environment in Alaska is an endless bounty of interesting and inspiring things to experience. Start free and be mindful of what you want to pay for. Potential savings: $200.

Book flights Ahead
Book eight weeks ahead for the lowest prices on outward flights. Potential savings: $100

Breakdown

Get from the air port	The number 7 bus travels between the downtown transit center (6th ave, between H and G streets) and the domestic (south) terminal hourly. Monday through Friday the service starts around 6:45am and operates until approximately 10pm. Car/RV rentals ARE MORE expensive at the airport. Don't rent there.
Get Around	RV for $120 a night from Outdoorsy.
Stay	Airbnbs and Vrbo's are considerably cheaper than hostels and hotels. RV's are the best option for seeing the real Alaska.
Eat	Seafood - delicious and cheaper than the states.
Do	Fairbanks island hop with a pilot delivering mail.
Sunset	Potter Marsh in Anchorage.
Best Budget Experiences	Alaska Heritage museum - When you arrive at this, you might think you made a mistake, as it is located inside a Wells Fargo Bank branch.
Cheapest Onward Destination	Seattle $50.

PRACTICAL THINGS TO REMEMBER TO SAVE MONEY

- Source your packing list items from thrift shops to save money.
- Book you accommodation or contact your RV hosts before you travel.
- Book the state ferry before you travel.
- Book train tickets if you plan to travel by train.
- Buy the discount coupons/app dependent on which attractions you plan to visit. If you plan to see all Alaska has to offer buy a coupon book - for $79.95, you get more than $15,000 in discounts.
- Download google maps for offline use in Alaska and Costco and Walmarts supermarket - there the cheapest.
- Go in April/May for the best prices and best weather. May is best as its the start of tourist season and you'll find more tours and day cruises are available. from Memorial to Labor days are our high season and everything tourism related will be 3x what it is.
- Alaska airlines have roundtrip cheap flights. Fly out of Chicago for $100 or less in May.
- The most affordable accommodations are in Seward.
- There is 23 hours of daylight in the summer - bring an eye mask for all travellers in your group.
- Really consider renting an RV. This alone can save you thou-sands and greatly enrich your Alaska experience. You can park anywhere that isn't private property, so if you see a nice river or lake or mountain view that you like, you can park there
overnight or for a few nights. It's cheaper than renting a car and then staying in hotels. Plus, you can buy groceries and save on dining out.
- Pick up a wild berry book and go berry picking. Berries are abundant in KENAI PENINSULA, obviously only in summer.
- Avoid over-scheduling. You don't want to pack so much into your trip you wind up feeling like you're working on the

conveyor belt called best sights of Alaska instead of fully saturating your senses in the incredible sights, sounds and smells of Alaskan nature.

FREQUENTLY ASKED QUESTIONS

1. Is it safe to travel Alaska alone?
Absolutely. Just come prepared for the extreme conditions.

2. Is bear spray useful when hiking and camping in Alaska?
Your chances of seeing one are extremely low unless you are planning to camp or hike in remote regions. If you're nervous about bears, bring bear spray and make noise if you fear one is near.

3. What is unique about Alaska in comparison to other countries?
The raw and uncompromising terrain.

4. How is Alaska different to the USA?
Alaska was a part of Russia since 1733. The British conquered Canada in 1760. In 1867, the Russians sold Alaska to the United States for 7.2 million dollars.

5. How can I save money on tours?
If you're taking a cruise in Alaska, shore excursion expenses can add up. Booking your own tours independently can easily save you hundreds of dollars. Visit each port's official tourism website for information on independent tour operators. It will give you an idea of what's available in each port and will help you stay within budget.

Money Mistakes in Alaska

Cost	Impact	Solution	Note
Booking tours to see everything	Tours are big business in Alaska averaging at $150 a tour.	You can do a lot of DIY tours when you don't need a boat	Or use coupon books for buying Alaskan tours.
Using your home currency (for non-Americans)	Some credit card rates charge for every transaction in another currency. Check carefully before you use it	Use a prepaid currency card like Wise Multi-Currency Debit Card where you can easily convert euros, pounds etc into USD.	
Buying bottled water	At $2.30 a bottle, this is a cost that can mount up quickly	Refill from the tap. Bring an on the go water filter bottle like Water-to-go.	
Eating like a tourist	Eating at tourist traps can triple your bill. Choose wisely.	Star cheap eats on google maps so you're never far from one.	
Forgetting essentials	Because of Alaksa's remoteness, essential items like toothpaste can cost you much more than at home.	Pack your essentials to last the duration of your trip.	Buy your bear spray at Costco - its cheapest there.
Not agreeing a price of everything in advance	Taxi's and other unpriced services allow people to con you..	Agree the price beforehand to avoid unwanted bills	
Forgetting your camera	You can try to get Puffins, Wolves, Orca, Whales, Polar Bear, Arctic Fox and Lynx's on camera and sell those photos on sites like shutterstock.com	Try Shutterstock, Getty Images or such websites. They will list your pics and pay you as there are sold.	Make yourself money while you travel

The secret to saving HUGE amounts of money when travelling to Alaska is...

Your mindset. Money is an emotional topic, if you associate words like cheapskate, Miser (and its £9.50 to go into Charles Dickens Alaska house, oh the Irony) with being thrifty when traveling you are likely to say 'F-it' and spend your money needlessly because you associate pain with saving money. You pay now for an immediate reward. Our brains are prehistoric; they focus on surviving day to day. Travel companies and hotels know this and put trillions into making you believe you will be happier when you spend on their products or services. Our poor brains are up against outdated programming and an onslaught of advertisements bombarding us with the message: spending money on travel equals PLEASURE. To correct this carefully lodged propaganda in your frontal cortex, you need to imagine your future self.

Saving money does not make you a cheapskate. It makes you smart. How do people get rich? They invest their money. They don't go out and earn it; they let their money earn more money. So every time you want to spend money, imagine this: while you travel, your money is working for you, not you for money. While you sleep, the money, you've invested is going up and up. That's a pleasure a pricey entrance fee can't give you. Thinking about putting your money to work for you tricks your brain into believing you are not withholding pleasure from yourself, you are saving your money to invest so you can go to even more amazing places. You are thus turning thrifty travel into a pleasure fueled sport.

When you've got money invested - If you want to splash your cash on a first-class airplane seat - you can. I can't tell you how to invest your money, only that you should. Saving $20 on taxis doesn't seem like much, but over time you could save upwards of $15,000 a year, which is a deposit for a house which you can rent on Airbnb to finance more travel. Your brain making money looks like your brain on cocaine, so tell yourself saving money is making money.

Scientists have proved that imagining your future self is the easiest way to associate pleasure with saving money. You can download FaceApp — which will give you a picture of what you will look like older and grayer, or you can take a deep breath just before spending money and ask yourself if you will regret the purchase later.

The easiest ways to waste money traveling are:

Getting a taxi. The solution to this is to always download the google map before you go. Many taxi drivers will drive you around for 15 minutes when the place you were trying to get to is a 5-minute walk... remember while not getting an overpriced taxi to tell yourself, 'I am saving money to free myself for more travel.' Spending money on overpriced food when hungry. The solution: carry snacks. A banana and an apple will cost you, in most places, less than a dollar.

Spending on entrance fees to top-rated attractions. If you really want to do it, spend the money happily. If you're conflicted, sleep on it. I don't regret spending $200 on a sky dive over the Great Barrier Reef; I regret going to the top of the shard on a cloudy day in London for $60. Only you can know, but make sure it's your decision and not the marketing directors at said top-rated attraction.

Telling yourself 'you only have the chance to see/eat/experience it now'. While this might be true, make sure YOU WANT to spend the money. Money spent is money you can't invest, and often you can have the same experience for much less.

You can experience luxurious travel on a small budget, which will trick your brain into thinking you're already a high-roller, which will mean you'll be more likely to act like one and invest your money. Stay in five-star hotels for $5 by booking on the day of your stay on booking.com to enjoy last-minute deals. You can go to fancy restaurants using daily deal sites. Ask your airline about last-minute upgrades to first-class or business. I paid $100 extra on a $179 ticket to Cuba from Germany to be bumped to Business Class. When you ask, it will surprise you what you can get both at hotels and airlines.

Travel, as the saying goes, is the only thing you spend money on that makes you richer. You can easily waste money, making it difficult to enjoy that metaphysical wealth. The biggest money saving secret is to turn bargain hunting into a pleasurable activity, not an annoyance. Budgeting consciously can be fun, don't feel disappointed because you don't spend the $60 to go into an attraction. Feel good because soon that $60 will soon earn money for you. Meaning, you'll have the time and money to enjoy more metaphysical wealth while your bank balance increases.

MAP of key attractions

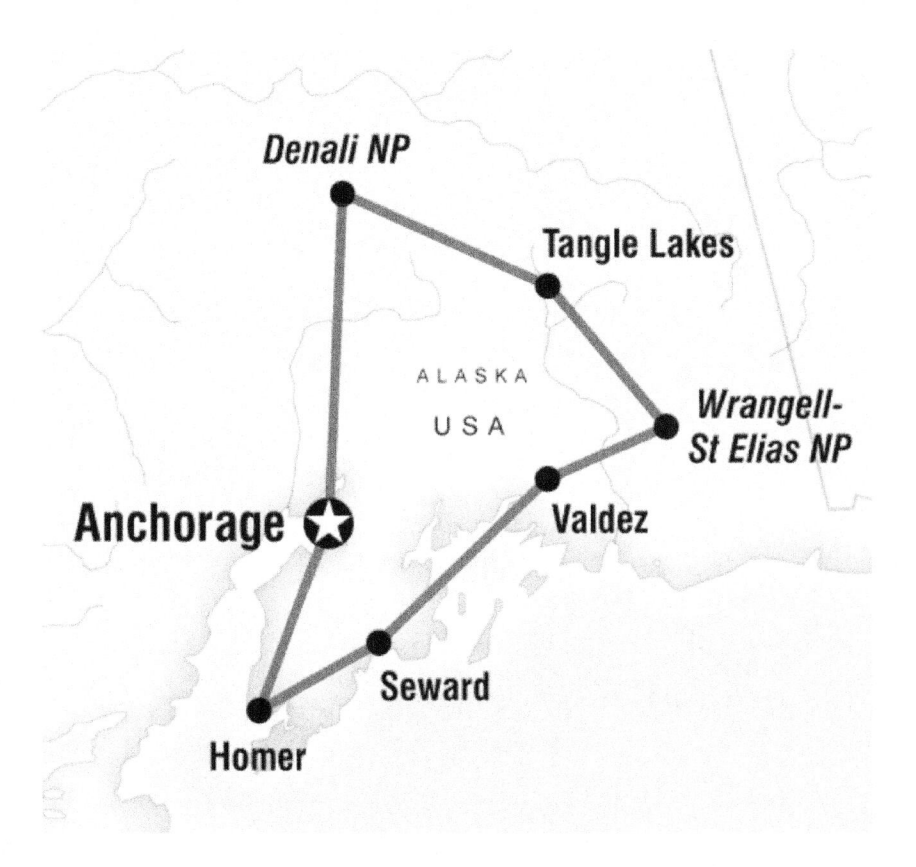

RV Route MAP

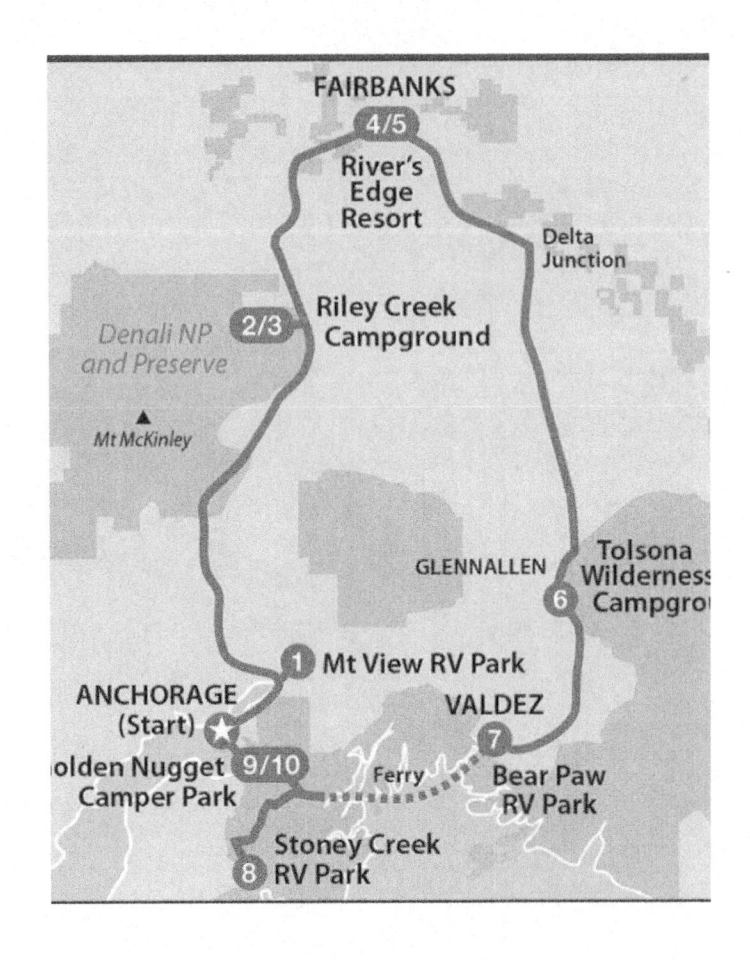

Alaska Train Map

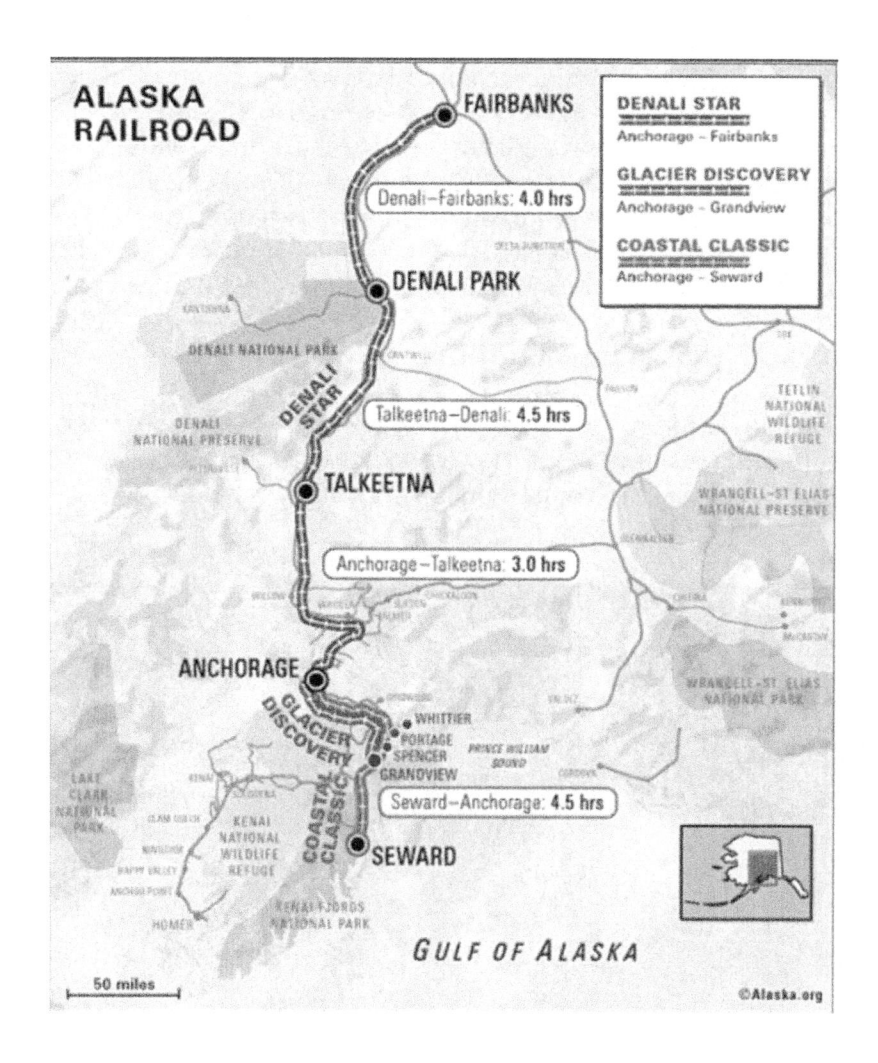

ALASKA RAILROAD

- **DENALI STAR** — Anchorage – Fairbanks
- **GLACIER DISCOVERY** — Anchorage – Grandview
- **COASTAL CLASSIC** — Anchorage – Seward

Denali–Fairbanks: 4.0 hrs
Talkeetna–Denali: 4.5 hrs
Anchorage–Talkeetna: 3.0 hrs
Seward–Anchorage: 4.5 hrs

GULF OF ALASKA

50 miles

©Alaska.org

So there it is. You can save a small fortune by being strategic with your trip planning. We've arranged everything in the guide to offer the best bang for your buck. Which means we took the view that if it's not an excellent investment for your money, we wouldn't include it. Why would a guide called 'Super Cheap' include lots of overpriced attractions? That said, if you think we've missed something or have unanswered questions, ping me an email: philgtang@gmail.com I'm on central Europe time and usually reply within 8 hours of getting your mail. We like to think of our guide books as evolving organisms helping our readers travel better cheaper. We use reader questions via email to update this book year round so you'll be helping other readers and yourself.

Don't put your dreams off!

Time is a currency you never get back and travel is its greatest return on investment. Plus, now you know you can visit Alaska for a fraction of the price most would have you believe.

Thank you for reading

Dear **Lovely Reader**,

If you have found this book useful, please consider writing a quick review on Amazon.

One person from every 1000 readers leaves a review on Amazon. It would mean more than you could ever know if you were one of our 1 in 1000 people to take the time to write a brief review.

Thank you so much for reading again and for spending your time and investing your trips future in Super Cheap Insider Guides. One last note, please don't listen to anyone who says 'Oh no, you can't visit Alaska on a budget'. Unlike you, they didn't have this book. You can do ANYWHERE on a budget with the right insider advice and planning. Sure, learning to travel to Alaska on a budget that doesn't compromise on anything or drastically compromise on safety or comfort levels is a skill, but this guide has done the detective work for you. Now it is time for you to put the advice into action.

Phil and the Super Cheap Insider Guides Team

P.S If you need any more super cheap tips we'd love to hear from you e-mail me at philgtang@gmail.com, we have a lot of contacts in every region, so if there's a specific bargain you're hunting we can help you find it.

DISCOVER YOUR NEXT VACATION

☑ **LUXURY ON A BUDGET APPROACH**
☑ **CHOOSE FROM 107 DESTINATIONS**
☑ **EACH BOOK PACKED WITH REAL-TIME LOCAL TIPS**

All are available in Paperback and e-book on Amazon: https://www.amazon.com/dp/B09C2DHQG5

Several are available as audiobooks. You can watch excerpts of ALL for FREE on YouTube: https://youtube.com/channel/UCxo9YV8-M9P1cFosU-Gjnqg

Bonus Travel Hacks

I've included these bonus travel hacks to help you plan and enjoy your trip to Alaska cheaply, joyfully, and smoothly. Perhaps they will even inspire you to start or renew a passion for long-term travel.

Common pitfalls when it comes to allocating money to <u>your desires</u> while traveling

Beware of Malleable mental accounting

Let's say you budgeted spending only $30 per day in Alaska but then you say well if I was at home I'd be spending $30 on food as an everyday purchase so you add another $30 to your budget. Don't fall into that trap as the likelihood is you still have expenses at home even if its just the cost of keeping your freezer going.

Beware of impulse purchases in Alaska

Restaurants that you haven't researched and just idle into can sometimes turn out to be great, but more often, they turn out to suck, especially if they are near tourist attractions. Make yourself a travel itinerary including where you'll eat breakfast and lunch. Dinner is always more expensive, so the meal best to enjoy at home or as a takeaway. This book is full of incredible cheap eats. All you have to do is plan to go to them.

Social media and FOMO (Fear of Missing Out)

'The pull of seeing acquaintances spend money on travel can often be a more powerful motivator to spend more while traveling than seeing an advertisement.' Beware of what you allow to influence you and go back to the question, what's the best money I can spend today?

Now-or-never sales strategies

One reason tourists are targeted by salespeople is the success of the now-or-never strategy. If you don't spend the money now… your never get the opportunity again. Rarely is this true.

Instead of spending your money on something you might not actually desire, take five minutes. Ask yourself, do I really want this? And return to the answer in five minutes. Your body will either say an absolute yes with a warm, excited feeling or a no with a weak, obscure feeling.

Unexpected costs

"Holding on to anger is like grasping a hot coal with the intent of throwing it at someone else; you only hurt yourself." The Buddha.

One downside to traveling is unexpected costs. When these spring up from airlines, accommodation providers, tours and on and on, they feel like a punch in the gut. During the pandemic my earnings fell to 20% of what they are normally. No one was traveling, no one was buying travel guides. My accountant out of nowhere significantly raised his fee for the year despite the fact there was a lot less money to count. I was so angry I consulted a lawyer who told me you will spend more taking him to court than you will paying his bill. I had to get myself into a good feeling place before I paid his bill, so I googled how to feel good paying someone who has scammed you.

The answer: Write down that you will receive 10 times the amount you are paying from an unexpected source. I did that. Four months later, the accountant wrote to me. He had applied for a COVID subsidy for me and I would receive... you guessed it almost exactly 10 times his fee.

Make of that what you want. I don't wish to get embroiled in a conversation about what many term 'woo-woo', but the result of my writing that I would receive 10 times the amount made me feel much, much better when paying him. And ultimately, that was a gift in itself. So next time some airline or train operator or hotel/ Airbnb sticks you with an unexpected fee, immediately write that you will receive 10 times the amount you are paying from an unexpected source. Rise your vibe and skip the added price of feeling angry.

Hack your allocations for your Alaska Trip

"The best trick for saving is to eliminate the decision to save." Perry Wright of Duke University.

Put the money you plan to spend in Alaska on a pre-paid card in the local currency. This cuts out two problems - not knowing how much you've spent and totally avoiding expensive currency conversion fees.

You could even create separate spaces. This much for transportation, this for tours/entertainment, accommodation and food. We are reluctant to spend money that is pre-assigned to categories or uses.

Write that you want to enjoy a $3,000 trip for $500 to your Alaska trip. Countless research shows when you put goals in writing, you have a higher chance of following through.

Spend all the money you want to on buying experiences in Alaska

> "Experiences are like good relatives that stay for a while and then leave. Objects are like relatives who move in and stay past their welcome." Daniel Gilbert, psychologist from Harvard University.

Economic and psychological research shows we are happier buying brief experiences on vacation rather than buying stuff to wear so give yourself freedom to spend on experiences knowing that the value you get back is many many times over.

Make saving money a game

There's one day a year where all the thrift shops where me and my family live sell everything there for a $1. My wife and I hold a contest where we take $5 and buy an entire outfit for each other. Whoever's outfit is liked more wins. We also look online to see whose outfit would have cost more to buy new. This year, my wife even snagged me an Armani coat for $1. I liked the coat when she showed it to me, but when I found out it was $500 new; I liked it and wore it a lot more.

Quadruple your money

Every-time you want to spend money, imagine it quadrupled. So the $10 you want to spend is actually $40. Now imagine that what you want to buy is four times the price. Do you still want it? If yes, go enjoy. If not, you've just saved yourself money, know you can choose to invest it in a way that quadruples or allocate it to something you really want to give you a greater return.

Understand what having unlimited amounts of money to spend in Alaska actually looks like

Let's look at what it would be like to have unlimited amounts of money to spend on your trip to Alaska.

Isolation

You take a private jet to your private Alaska hotel. There you are lavished with the best food, drink, and entertainment. Spending vast amounts of money on vacation equals being isolated.

If you're on your honeymoon and you want to be alone with your Amore, this is wonderful, but it can be equally wonderful to make new friends. Know this a study 'carried out by Brigham Young University, Utah found that while obesity increased risk of death by 30%, loneliness increased it by half.'

Comfort

Money can buy you late check outs of five-star hotels and priority boarding on airlines, all of which add up to comfort. But as this book has shown you, saving money in Alaska doesn't minimize comfort, that's just a lie travel agencies littered with glossy brochures want you to believe.

You can do late-check outs for free with the right credit cards and priority boarding can be purchased with a lot of airlines from $4. If you want to go big with first-class or business, flights offset your own travel costs by renting your own home or you can upgrade at the airport often for a fraction of what you would have paid booking a business flight online.

MORE TIPS TO FIND CHEAP FLIGHTS

"The use of travelling is to regulate imagination by reality, and instead of thinking how things may be, to see them as they are." Samuel Jackson

If you're working full-time, you can save yourself a lot of money by requesting your time off from work starting in the middle of the week. Tuesdays and Wednesdays are the cheapest days to fly. You can save thousands just by adjusting your time off.

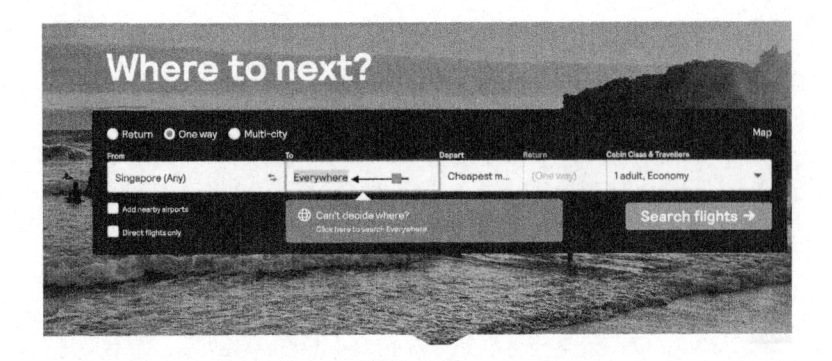

The simplest secret to booking cheap flights is open parameters. Let's say you want to fly from Chicago to Paris. You enter the USA in from and select France under to. You may find flights from New York City to Paris for $70. Then you just need to find a cheap flight to NYC. Make sure you calculate full costs, including if you need airport accommodation and of course getting to and from airports, **but in nearly every instance open parameters will save you at least half the cost of the flight.**

If you're not sure about where you want to go, use open parameters to show you the cheapest destinations from your city. Start with skyscanner.net they include the low-cost airlines that others like Kayak leave out. Google Flights can also show you cheap destinations. To see these leave the WHERE TO section blank.

Open parameters can also show you the cheapest dates to fly. If you're flexible, you can save up to 80% of the flight cost. Always check the weather at your destination before you book. Sometimes a $400 flight will be $20, because it's monsoon season. But hey, if you like the rain, why not?

ALWAYS USE A PRIVATE BROWSER TO BOOK FLIGHTS

Skyscanner and other sites track your IP address and put prices up and down based on what they determine your strength of conviction to buy. e.g. if you've booked one-way and are looking for the return, these sites will jack the prices up by in most cases 50%. Incognito browsing pays.

Use a VPN such as Hola to book your flight from your destination

Install Hola, change your destination to the country you are flying to. The location from which a ticket is booked can affect the price significantly as algorithms consider local buying power.

Choose the right time to buy your ticket.

Choose the right time to buy your ticket, as purchasing tickets on a Sunday has been proven to be cheaper. If you can only book during the week, try to do it on a Tuesday.

Mistake fares

Email alerts from individual carriers are where you can find the best 'mistake fares". This is where a computer error has resulted in an airline offering the wrong fare. In my experience, it's best to sign up to individual carriers email lists, but if you ARE lazy Secret Flying puts together a daily roster of mistake fares. Visit https://www.secretflying.com/errorfare/ to see if there're any errors that can benefit you.

Fly late for cheaper prices

Red-eye flights, the ones that leave later in the day, are typically cheaper and less crowded, so aim to book that flight if possible. You will also get through the airport much quicker at the end of the day. Just make sure there's ground transport available for when you land. You don't want to save $50 on the airfare and spend it on a taxi to your accommodation.

Use this APP for same day flights

If your plans are flexible, use 'Get The Flight Out' (http://www.gtfoflights.com/) a fare tracker Hopper that shows you same-day deeply discounted flights. This is best for long-haul flights with major carriers. You can often find a British Airways round-trip from JFK Airport to Heathrow for $300. If you booked this in advance, you'd pay at least double.

Take an empty water bottle with you

Airport prices on food and drinks are sky high. It disgusts me to see some airports charging $10 for a bottle of water. ALWAYS take an empty water bottle with you. It's relatively unknown, but most airports have drinking water fountains past the security check. Just type in your airport name to wateratairports.com to locate the fountain. Then once you've passed security (because they don't allow you to take 100ml or more of liquids) you can freely refill your bottle with water.

Round-the-World (RTW) Tickets

It is always cheaper to book your flights using a DIY approach. First, you may decide you want to stay longer in one country, and a RTW will charge you a hefty fee for changing your flight. Secondly, it all depends on where and when you travel and as we have discussed, there are many ways to ensure you pay way less than $1,500 for a year of flights. If you're travelling long-haul, the best strategy is to buy a return ticket, say New York, to Bangkok and then take cheap flights or transport around Asia and even to Australia and beyond.

Cut your costs to and from airports

Don't you hate it when getting to and from the airport is more expensive than your flight! And this is true in so many cities, especially European ones. For some reason, Google often shows the most expensive options. Use Omio to compare the cheapest transport options and save on airport transfer costs.

Car sharing instead of taxis

Check if Alaska has car sharing at the airport. Often they'll be tons of cars parked at the airport that are half the price of taking a taxi into the city. In most instances, you register your driving licence on an app and scan the code on the car to get going.

Checking Bags

Sometimes you need to check bags. If you do, put an AirTag inside. That way, you'll be about to see when you land where your bag is. This saves you the nail biting wait at baggage claim. And if worse comes to worst, and you see your bag is actually in another city, you can calmly stroll over to customer services and show them where your bag is.

Is it cheaper and more convenient to send your bags ahead?

Before you check your bags, check if it's cheaper to send them ahead of you with sendmybag.com obviously if you're staying in an Airbnb, you'll need to ask the hosts permission or you can time them to arrive the day after you. Hotels are normally very amenable.

What Credit Card Gives The Best Air Miles?

You can slash the cost of flights just for spending on a piece of plastic.

LET'S TALK ABOUT DEBT

Before we go into the best cards for each country, let's first talk about debt. The US system offers the best and biggest rewards. Why? Because they rely on the fact that many people living in the US will not pay their cards in full and the card will earn the bank significant interest payments. Other countries have a very different attitude towards money, debt, and saving than Americans. Thus in Germany and Austria the offerings aren't as favourable as the UK, Spain and Australia, where debt culture is more widely embraced. The takeaway here is this: **Only spend on one of these cards when you have set-up an automatic total monthly balance repayment. Don't let banks profit from your lizard brain!**

The best air-mile credit cards for those living in the UK

Amex Preferred Rewards Gold comes out top for those living in the UK for 2023.

Here are the benefits:

- 20,000-point bonus on £3,000 spend in first three months. These can be used towards flights with British Airways, Virgin Atlantic, Emirates and Etihad, and often

other rewards, such as hotel stays and car hire.
- 1 point per £1 spent
- 1 point = 1 airline point
- Two free visits a year to airport lounges
- No fee in year one, then £140/yr

The downside:

- Fail to repay fully and it's 59.9% rep APR interest, incl fee

You'll need to cancel before the £140/yr fee kicks in year two if you want to avoid it.

The best air-mile credit cards for those living in Canada

Aeroplan is the superior rewards program in Canada. The card has a high earn rate for Aeroplan Points, generating 1.5 points per $1 spent on eligible purchases. Look at the specifics of the eligible purchases https://www.aircanada.com/ca/en/aco/home/aeroplan/earn.html. If you're not spending on these things AMEX's Membership Rewards program offers you the best returns in Canada.

The best air-mile credit cards for those living in Germany

If you have a German bank account, you can apply for a Lufthansa credit card.

Earn 50,000 award miles if you spend $3,000 in purchases and paying the annual fee, both within the first 90 days.

Earn 2 award miles per $1 spent on ticket purchases directly from Miles & More integrated airline partners.

Earn 1 award mile per $1 spent on all other purchases.

The downsides

the €89 annual fee

Limited to fly with Lufthansa and its partners but you can capitalise on perks like the companion pass and airport lounge vouchers.

You need excellent credit to get this card.

The best air-mile credit cards for those living in Austria

"In Austria, Miles & More offers you a special credit card. You get miles for each purchase with the credit card. The Miles & More program calculates miles earned based on the distance flown and booking class. For European flights, the booking class is a flat rate. For intercontinental flights, mileage is calculated by multiplying the booking class by the distance flown." They offer a calculator so you can see how many points you could earn: https://www.miles-and-more.com/at/en/earn/airlines/mileage-calculator.html

The best air-mile credit cards for those living in Spain:

"The American Express card is the best known and oldest to earn miles, thanks to its membership Rewards program. When making payments with this card, points are added, which can then be exchanged for miles from airlines such as Iberia, Air Europa, Emirates or Alitalia." More information is available here: https://www.americanexpress.com/es-es/

The best air-mile credit cards for those living in Australia

ANZ Rewards Black comes out top for 2023.

180,000 bonus ANZ Reward Points (can get an $800 gift card) and $0 annual fee for the first year with the ANZ Rewards Black
Points Per Spend: 1 Velocity point on purchases of up to

$5,000 per statement period and 0.5 Velocity points thereafter.
Annual Fee: $0 in the first year, then $375 after.
Ns no set minimum income required, however, there is a minimum credit limit of $15,000 on this card.

Here are some ways you can hack points onto this card:
https://www.pointhacks.com.au/credit-cards/anz-rewards-black-guide/

The best air-mile credit card solution for those living in the USA with a POOR credit score

The downside to Airline Mile cards is that they require good or excellent credit scores, meaning 690 or higher.

If you have bad credit and want to use credit card air lines you will need to rebuild your credit poor. The Credit One Bank® Platinum Visa® for Rebuilding Credit is a good credit card for people with bad credit who don't want to place a deposit on a secured card. The Credit One Platinum Visa offers a $300 credit limit, rewards, and the potential for credit-limit increases, which in time will help rebuild your score.

PLEASE don't sign-up for any of these cards if you can't trust yourself to repay it in full monthly. This will only lead to stress for you.

Frequent Flyer Memberships

"Points" and "miles" are often used interchangeably, but they're usually two very different things. Maximise and diversify your rewards by utilising both.

A frequent-flyer program (FFP) is a loyalty program offered by an airline. They are designed to encourage airline customers to fly more to accumulate points (also called miles, kilometres, or segments) which can be redeemed for air travel or other rewards.

You can sign up with any FFP program for free. There are three major airline alliances in the world: Oneworld, SkyTeam and Star Alliance. I am with One World https://www.oneworld.com/members because the points can be accrued and used for most flights.

The best return on your points is to use them for international business or first class flights with lie-flat seats. You would need 3 times more miles compared to an economy flight, but if you paid cash, you'd pay 5 - 10 times more than the cost of the economy flight, so it really pays to use your points only for upgrades. The worst value for your miles is to buy an economy seat or worse, a gift from the airlines gift-shop.

Sign up for a family/household account to pool miles together. If you share a common address, you can claim the miles with most airlines. You can use AwardWallet to keep track of your miles. Remember that they only last for 2 years, so use them before they expire.

How to get 70% off a Cruise

An average cruise can set you back $4,000. If you dream of cruising the oceans, but find the pricing too high, look at repositioning cruises. You can save as much as 70% by taking a cruise which takes the boat back to its home port.

These one-way itineraries take place during low cruise seasons when ships have to reposition themselves to locations where there's warmer weather.

To find a repositioning cruise, go to vacationstogo.com/repositioning_cruises.cfm. This simple and often overlooked booking trick is great for avoiding long flights with children and can save you so much money!

It's worth noting we don't have any affiliations with any travel service or provider. The links we suggest are chosen based on our experience of finding the best deals.

Pack like a Pro

"He who would travel happily must travel light." – Antoine de St. Exupery 59.

Travel as lightly as you can. We always need less than we think. You will be very grateful that you have a light pack when changing trains, travelling through the airport, catching a bus, walking to your accommodation, or climbing stairs.

Make a list of what you will wear for 7 days and take only those clothes. You can easily wash your things while you're travelling if you stay in an Airbnb with a washing machine or visit a local laundrette. Roll your clothes for maximum space usage and fewer wrinkles. If you feel really nervous about travelling with such few things, make sure you have a dressier outfit, a little black dress for women is always valuable, a shirt for men. Then pack shorts, a long pair of pants, loose tops and a hoodie to snuggle in. Remind yourself that a lack of clothing options is an opportunity to find bargain new outfits in thrift stores. You can either sell these on eBay after you've worn them or post them home to yourself. You'll feel less stressed, as you don't have to look after or feel weighed down by excess baggage. Here are three things to remember when packing:

- Co-ordinate colours - make sure everything you bring can be worn together.

- Be happy to do laundry - fresh clothes when you're travelling feels very luxurious.

- Take liquid minis no bigger than 60ml. Liquid is heavy, and you simply don't need to carry so much at one time.

- Buy reversible clothes (coats are a great idea), dresses which can be worn multiple different ways.

Checks to Avoid Fees

Always have 6 months' validity on your passport

To enter most countries, you need 6 months from the day you land. Factor in different time zones around the world if your passport is on the edge. Airport security will stop you from boarding your flight at the airport if your passport has 5 months and 29 days left.

Google Your Flight Number before you leave for the airport

Easily find out where your plane is from anywhere. Confirm the status of your flight before you leave for the airport with flightaware.com. This can save you long unnecessary wait times.

Check-in online

The founder, Ryan O'Leary of budget airline Ryanair famously said: "We think they should pay €60 for [failing to check-in online] being so stupid.". Always check-in online, even for international flights. Cheaper international carriers like Scoot will charge you at the airport to check-in.

Checking Bags

Never, ever check a bag if you can avoid it. Sometimes you need to check bags. If you do, put an AirTag inside. That way, you'll be about to see when you land where your bag is. This saves you the nail biting wait at baggage claim. And if worse comes to worst, and you see your bag is actually in another city, you can calmly stroll over to customer services and show them where your bag is.

Is it cheaper and more convenient to send your bags ahead?

Before you check your bags, check if it's cheaper to send them ahead of you with sendmybag.com obviously if you're staying in an Airbnb, you'll need to ask the hosts permission or you can time them to arrive the day after you. Hotels are normally very amenable.

It is always cheaper to put heavier items on a ship, rather than take them on a flight with you. Find the best prices for shipping at https://www.parcelmonkey.com/delivery-services/shipping-heavy-items

Use a fragile sticker

Put a 'Fragile' sticker on anything you check to ensure that it's handled better as it goes through security. It'll also be one of the first bags released after the flight, getting you out of the airport quicker.

If you check your bag, photograph it

Take a photo of your bag before you check it. This will speed up the paperwork if it is damaged or lost.

Relaxing at the Airport

The best way to relax at the airport is in a lounge where they provide free food, drinks, comfortable chairs, luxurious amenities (many have showers) and, if you're lucky, a peaceful ambience. If you're there for a longer time, look for Airport Cubicles, sleep pods which charge by the hour.

You can use your FFP Card (Frequent Flyer Memberships) to get into select lounges for free. Check your eligibility before you pay.

If you're travelling a lot, I'd recommend investing in a [Priority Pass](#) for the airport.

It includes 850-plus airport lounges around the world. The cost is $99 for the year and $27 per lounge visit or you can pay $399 for the year all inclusive.

If you need a lounge for a one-off day, you can get a Day Pass. Buy it online for a discount, it always works out cheaper than buying at the airport. Use www.LoungePass.com.

Lounges are also great if you're travelling with kids, as they're normally free for kids and will definitely cost you less than snacks for your little ones. The rule is that kids should be seen and not heard, so consider this before taking an overly excited child who wants to run around, or you might be asked to leave even after you've paid.

How to spend money

Bank ATM fees vary from $2.50 per transaction to as high as $5 or more, depending on the ATM and the country. You can completely skip those fees by paying with card and using a card which can hold multiple currencies.

Budget travel hacking begins with a strategy to spend without fees. Your individual strategy depends on the country you legally reside in as to what cards are available. Happily there are some fin-tech solutions which can save you thousands on those pesky ATM withdrawal fees and are widely available globally. Here are a selection of cards you can pre-charge with currency for Alaska:

N26

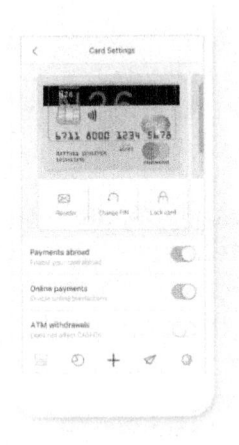

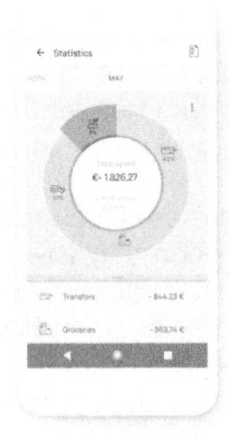

N26 is a 12-year-old digital bank. I have been using them for over 6 years. The key advantage is fee-free card transactions abroad. They have a very elegant app, where you can check your timeline for all transactions listed in real time or manage your in-app security anywhere. The card you receive is a Mastercard so you can use it everywhere. If you lose the card, you don't have to call anyone, just open the app and swipe 'lock card'. It puts your purchases into a graph automatically so you can see what you spend on. You can open an account from abroad entirely online, all you need is your passport and a camera n26.com

Revolut

Revolut is a multi-currency account that allows you to hold and exchange 29 currencies and spend fee-free abroad. It's a UK based neobank, but accepts customers from all over the world.

Wise debit card

If you're going to be in one place for a long time, the Wise debit card is like having your travel money on a card – it lets you spend money at the real exchange rate.

Monzo

Monzo is good if your UK based. They offer a fee-free UK account. Fee-free international money transfers and fee-free spending abroad.

The downside

The cards above are debit cards, meaning you need to have money in those accounts to spend it. This comes with one big downside: safety. Credit card issuers' have "zero liability" meaning you're not liable for unauthorised charges. All the cards listed above do provide cover for unauthorised charges but times vary greatly in how quickly you'd get your money back if it were stolen.

The best option is to check in your country to see which credit cards are the best for travelling and set up monthly payments to repay the whole amount so you don't pay unnecessary interest. In the USA, Schwab regularly ranks at the top for travel credit cards. Credit cards are always the safer option when abroad simply because you get your money back faster if its stolen and if you're renting cars, most will give you free insurance when you book the car rental using the card, saving you money.

Always withdraw money; never exchange.

Money exchanges, whether they be on the streets or in the airports will NEVER give you a good exchange rate. Do not bring bundles of cash. Instead, withdraw local currency from the ATM as needed and try to use only free ATMs. Many in airports charge you a fee to withdraw cash. Look for bigger ATMs attached to banks to avoid this.

Recap

- Take cash from local, non-charging ATMs for the best rates.

- Never change at airport exchange desks unless you absolutely have to, then just change just enough to be able get to a bank ATM.

- Bring a spare credit card for emergencies.

- Split cash in various places on your person (pockets, shoes) and in your luggage. It's never sensible to keep your cash or cards all in one place.

- In higher risk areas, use a money belt under your clothes or put $50 in your shoe or bra.

Revolut
Revolut is a multi-currency account that allows you to hold and exchange 29 currencies and spend fee-free abroad. It's a UK based neobank, but accepts customers from all over the world.

Wise debit card
If you're going to be in one place for a long time the Wise debit card is like having your travel money on a card – it lets you spend money at the real exchange rate.

Monzo
Monzo is good if your UK based. They offer a fee-free UK account. Fee-free international money transfers and fee-free spending abroad.

The downside

The cards above are debit cards, meaning you need to have money in those accounts to spend it. This comes with one big downside: safety. Credit card issuers' have "zero liability" meaning you're not liable for unauthorised charges. All of the cards listed above do provide cover for unauthorised charges but times vary greatly in how quickly you'd get your money back if it were stolen.

The best option is to check in your country to see which credit cards are the best for travelling and set up monthly payments to repay the whole amount so you don't pay unnecessary interest. In the USA, Schwab[2] regularly ranks at the top for travel credit cards. Credit cards are always the safer option when abroad simply because you get your

---

[2] Charles Schwab High Yield Checking accounts refund every single ATM fee worldwide, require no minimum balance and have no monthly fee.

money back faster if its stolen and if you're renting cars, most will give you free insurance when you book the car rental using the card, saving you money.

Always withdraw money; never exchange.

Money exchanges whether they be on the streets or in the airports will NEVER give you a good exchange rate. Do not bring bundles of cash. Instead withdraw local currency from the ATM as needed and try to use only free ATM's. Many in airports charge you a fee to withdraw cash. Look for bigger ATM's attached to banks to avoid this.

Recap

- Take cash from local, non-charging ATMs for the best rates.
- Never change at airport exchange desks unless you absolutely have to, then just change just enough to be able get to a bank ATM.
- Bring a spare credit card for emergencies.
- Split cash in various places on your person (pockets, shoes) and in your luggage. Its never sensible to keep your cash or cards all in one place.
- In higher risk areas, use a money belt under your clothes or put $50 in your shoe or bra.

How to save money while travelling

Saving money while travelling sounds like an oxymoron, but it can be done with little to no effort. Einstein is credited as saying, "Compound interest is the eighth wonder of the world." If you saved and invested $100 today, in 20 years, it would be $2,000 thanks to the power of compound interest. It makes sense then to save your money, invest and make even more money.

The Acorns app is a simple system for this. It rounds up your credit card purchases and puts the rest into a savings account. So if you pay for a coffee and its $3.01, you'll save 0.99 cents. You won't even notice you're saving by using this app: www.acorns.com

Here are some more generic ways you can always save money while travelling:

Device Safety

Having your phone, iPad or laptop stolen is one BIG and annoying way you can lose money travelling. The simple solution is to use apps to track your devices. Some OSes have this feature built-in. Prey will try your smartphones or laptops (preyproject.com).

Book New Airbnb's

When you take a risk on a new Airbnb listing, you save money. Just make sure the hosts profile is at least 3 years old and has reviews.

If you end up in an overcrowded city

The website https://campspace.com/ is like Airbnb for camping in people's garden and is a great way to save money if you end up in a city during a big event.

Look out for free classes

Lots of hostels offer free classes for guests. If you're planning to stay in a hostel, check out what classes your hostel offers. I have learnt languages, cooking techniques, dance styles, drawing and all manner of things for free by taking advantage of free classes at hostels.

Get student discounts

If you're studying buy an ISIC card - International Student Identity Card. It is internationally recognised, valid in 133 countries and offers more than 150,000 discounts!

Get Senior Citizen discounts

Most state run attractions, ie, museums, galleries will offer a discount for people over 65 with ID.

Instal maps.me

Maps me is extremely good for travelling without data. It's like offline google maps without the huge download size.

Always buy travel insurance

Don't travel without travel insurance. It is a small cost to pay compared with what could be a huge medical bill.

Travel Apps That'll Make Budget Travel Easier

Travel apps are useful for booking and managing travel logistics. They have one fatal downside: they can track you in the app and keep prices up. If you face this, access the site from an incognito browser tab.

Here are the best apps and what they can do for you:

- Best For flight Fare-Watching: Hopper.

- Best for booking flights: Skyscanner and Google Flights

- Best for timing airport arrivals: FlightAware - check on delays, cancellations and gate changes.

- Best for overcoming a fear of flying: SkyGuru - turbulence forecasts for the route you're flying.

- Best for sharing your location: TripWhistle - text or send your GPS coordinates or location easily.

- Best for splitting expenses among co-travellers: Splittr, Trip Splitter, Venmo or Splitwise.

How NOT to be ripped off

> "One of the great things about travel is that you find out how many good, kind people there are."
> — Edith Wharton

The quote above may seem ill placed in a chapter entitled how not to be ripped off, but I included it to remind you that the vast majority of people do not want to rip you off. In fact, scammers are normally limited to three situations:

1. Around heavily visited attractions - these places are targeted purposively due to sheer footfall. Many criminals believe ripping people off is simply a numbers game.

2. In cities or countries with low-salaries or communist ideologies. If they can't make money in the country, they seek to scam foreigners. If you have travelled to India, Morocco or Cuba you will have observed this phenomenon.

3. When you are stuck and the person helping you know you have limited options.

Scammers know that most people will avoid confrontation. Don't feel bad about utterly ignoring someone and saying no. Here are six strategies to avoid being ripped off:

1. **Never ever agree to pay as much as you want. Always decide on a price before.**

Whoever you're dealing with is trained to tell you, they are uninterested in money. This is a trap. If you let people do this they will ask for MUCH MORE money at the end, and because you have used there service, you will feel obliged to pay. This is a conman's trick and nothing more.

2. Pack light

You can move faster and easier. If you take heavy luggage, you will end up taking taxis which are comparatively very costly over time.

3. NEVER use the airport taxi service. Plan to use public transport before you reach the airport.

4. Don't buy a sim card from the airport. Buy from the local supermarkets it will cost 50% less.

5. Eat at local restaurants serving regional food

Food defines culture. Exploring all delights available to the palate doesn't need to cost enormous sums.

6. Ask the locals what something should cost, and try not to pay over that.

7. If you find yourself with limited options. e.g. your taxi dumps you on the side of the road because you refuse to pay more (common in India and parts of South America) don't act desperate and negotiate as if you have other options or you will be extorted.

8. Don't blindly rely on social media[3]

Let's say you post in a Facebook group that you want tips for travelling to The Maldives. A lot of the comments you will receive come from guides, hosts and restaurants doing their own promotion. It's estimated that 50% or more of

---

[3] https://arstechnica.com/tech-policy/2019/12/social-media-platforms-leave-95-of-reported-fake-accounts-up-study-finds/

Facebook's current monthly active users are fake. And what's worse, a recent study found Social media platforms leave 95% of reported fake accounts up. These accounts are the digital versions of the men who hang around the Grand Palace in Bangkok telling tourists its closed, to divert you to shops where they will receive a commission for bringing you.

It can also be the case that genuine comments come from people who have totally different interests, beliefs and yes, budgets to yours. Make your experience your own and don't believe every comment you read.

Bottom line: use caution when accepting recommendations on social media and always fact-check with your own research.

Small tweaks on the road add up to big differences in your bank balance

Take advantage of other hotel amenities

If you fancy a swim but you're nowhere near the ocean, try the nearest hotel with a pool. As long as you buy a drink, the hotel staff will probably grant you access.

Fill up your mini bar for free.

Fill up your mini bar for free by storing things from the breakfast bar or grocery shop in your mini bar to give you a greater selection of drinks and food without the hefty price tag.

Save yourself some ironing

Use the steam from the shower to get rid of wrinkles in clothing. If something is creased, leave it trapped with the steam in the bathroom overnight for even better results.

See somewhere else for free

Opt for long stopovers, allowing you to experience another city without spending much money.

Wear your heaviest clothes

On the plane to save weight in your pack, allowing you to bring more with you. Big coats can then be used as pillows to make your flight more comfortable.

Don't get lost while you're away.

Find where you want to go using Google Maps, then type 'OK Maps' into the search bar to store this information for offline viewing.

Use car renting services

Share Now or Car2Go allow you to hire a car for 2 hours for $25 in a lot of European countries.

Share Rides

Use sites like blablacar.com to find others who are driving in your direction. It can be 80% cheaper than normal transport. Just check the drivers reviews.

Use free gym passes

Get a free gym day pass by googling the name of a local gym and free day pass.

When asked by people providing you a service where you are from..

If there's no price list for the service you are asking for, when asked where you are from, Say you are from a lesser-known poorer country. I normally say Macedonia, and if they don't know where it is, add it's a poor country. If you say UK, USA, the majority of Europe bar the well-known poorer countries taxi drivers, tour operators etc will match the price to what they think you pay at home.

Set-up a New Uber/ other car hailing app account for discounts

By googling you can find offers with $50 free for new users in most cities for Uber/ Lyft/ Bolt and alike. Just set up a new gmail.com email account to take advantage.

Where and How to Make Friends

"People don't take trips, trips take people." – John Steinbeck

Become popular at the airport

Want to become popular at the airport? Pack a power bar with multiple outlets and just see how many friends you can make. It's amazing how many people forget their chargers, or who packed them in the luggage that they checked in.

Stay in Hostels

First of all, Hostels don't have to be shared dorms, and they cater to a much wider demographic than is assumed. Hostels are a better environment for meeting people than hotels, and more importantly, they tended to open up excursion opportunities that further opened up that opportunity.

Or take up a hobby

If hostels are a definite no-no for you; find an interest. Take up a hobby where you will meet people. I've dived for years and the nature of diving is you're always paired up with a dive buddy. I met a lot of interesting people that way.

Small tweaks on the road add up to big differences in your bank balance

Take advantage of other hotel's amenities

If you fancy a swim but you're nowhere near the ocean, try the nearest hotel with a pool. As long as you buy a drink, the hotel staff will likely grant you access.

Fill up your mini bar for free.

Fill up your mini bar for free by storing things from the breakfast bar or grocery shop in your mini bar to give you a greater selection of drinks and food without the hefty price tag.

Save yourself some ironing

Use the steam from the shower to get rid of wrinkles in clothing. If something is creased, leave it trapped with the steam in the bathroom overnight for even better results.

See somewhere else for free

Opt for long stopovers, allowing you to experience another city without spending much money.

Wear your heaviest clothes

on the plane to save weight in your pack, allowing you to bring more with you. Big coats can then be used as pillows to make your flight more comfortable.

Don't get lost while you're away.

Find where you want to go using Google Maps, then type 'OK Maps' into the search bar to store this information for offline viewing.

Use car renting services

Share Now or Car2Go allow you to hire a car for 2 hours for $25 in a lot of Europe.

Share Rides

Use sites like blablacar.com to find others who are driving in your direction. It can be 80% cheaper than normal transport. Just check the drivers reviews.

Use free gym passes

Get a free gym day pass by googling the name of a local gym and free day pass.

When asked by people providing you a service where you are from..

If there's no price list for the service you are asking for, when asked where you are from, Say you are from a lesser-known poorer country. I normally say Macedonia, and if they don't know where it is, add it's a poor country. If you say UK, USA, the majority of Europe bar the well-known poorer countries taxi drivers, tour operators etc will match the price to what they think you pay at home.

Set-up a New Uber/ other car hailing app account for discounts

By googling you can find offers with $50 free for new users in most cities for Uber/ Lyft/ Bolt and alike. Just set up a new gmail.com email account to take advantage.

Where and How to Make Friends

"People don't take trips, trips take people." – John Steinbeck

Become popular at the airport

Want to become popular at the airport? Pack a power bar with multiple outlets and just see how many friends you can make. It's amazing how many people forget their chargers, or who packed them in the luggage that they checked in.

Stay in Hostels

First of all, Hostels don't have to be shared dorms, and they cater to a much wider demographic than is assumed. Hostels are a better environment for meeting people than hotels, and more importantly they tended to open up excursion opportunities that further opened up that opportunity.

Or take up a hobby

If hostels are a definite no-no for you; find an interest. Take up a hobby where you will meet people. I've dived for years and the nature of diving is you're always paired up with a dive buddy. I met a lot of interesting people that way.

When unpleasantries come your way...

We all have our good and bad days travelling, and on a bad day you can feel like just taking a flight home. Here are some ways to overcome common travel problems:

Anxiety when flying

It has been over 40 years since a plane has been brought down by turbulence. Repeat that number to yourself: 40 years! Planes are built to withstand lighting strikes, extreme storms and ultimately can adjust course to get out of their way. Landing and take-off are when the most accidents happen, but you have statistically three times the chance of winning a huge jackpot lottery, then you do of dying in a plane crash.

If you feel afraid on the flight, focus on your breathing saying the word 'smooth' over and over until the flight is smooth. Always check the airline safety record on airlinerating.com I was surprised to learn Ryanair and Easyjet as much less safe than Wizz Air according to those ratings because they sell similarly priced flights. If there is extreme turbulence, I feel much better knowing I'm in a 7 star safety plane.

Wanting to sleep instead of seeing new places

This is a common problem. Just relax, there's little point doing fun things when you feel tired. Factor in jet-lag to your travel plans. When you're rested and alert you'll enjoy your new temporary home much more. Many people hate the first week of a long-trip because of jet-lag and often blame this on their first destination, but its rarely true. Ask travellers who 'hate' a particular place and you will see that very often they either had jet-lag or an unpleasant journey there.

Going over budget

Come back from a trip to a monster credit card bill? Hopefully, this guide has prevented you from returning to an unwanted bill. Of course, there are costs that can creep up and this is a reminder about how to prevent them making their way on to your credit card bill:

- To and from the airport. Solution: leave adequate time and take the cheapest method - book before.

- Baggage. Solution: take hand luggage and post things you might need to yourself.

- Eating out. Solution: go to cheap eats places and suggest those to friends.

- Parking. Solution: use apps to find free parking

- Tipping. Solution Leave a modest tip and tell the server you will write them a nice review.

- Souvenirs. Solution: fridge magnets only.

- Giving to the poor. (This one still gets me, but if you're giving away $10 a day - it adds up) Solution: volunteer your time instead and recognise that in tourist destinations many beggars are run by organised crime gangs.

Price v Comfort

I love traveling. I don't love struggling. I like decent accommodation, being able to eat properly and see places and enjoy. I am never in the mood for low-cost airlines or crappy transfers, so here's what I do to save money.

- Avoid organised tours unless you are going to a place where safety is a real issue. They are expensive and constrain your wanderlust to typical things. I only recommend them in Algeria, Iran and Papua New Guinea - where language and gender views pose serious problems all cured by a reputable tour organiser.

- Eat what the locals do.

- Cook in your Airbnb/ hostel where restaurants are expensive.

- Shop at local markets.

- Spend time choosing your flight, and check the operator on arilineratings.com

- Mix up hostels and Airbnbs. Hostels for meeting people, Airbnb for relaxing and feeling 'at home'.

Not knowing where free toilets are

Use Toilet Finder - https://play.google.com/store/apps/details?id=com.bto.toilet&hl=en

Your Airbnb is awful

Airbnb customer service is notoriously bad. Help yourself out. Try to sort things out with the host, but if you can't, take photos of everything e.g bed, bathroom, mess, doors, contact them within 24 hours. Tell them you had to leave and pay for new accommodation. Ask politely for a full refund including booking fees. With photographic evidence and your new accommodation receipt, they can't refuse.

The airline loses your bag

Go to the Luggage desk before leaving the airport and report the bag missing. Hopefully you've headed the advice to put an AirTag in your checked bag and you can show them where to find your bag. Most airlines will give you an overnight bag, ask where you're staying and return the bag to you within three days. It's extremely rare for Airlines to lose your bag due to technological innovation, but if that happens you should submit an insurance claim after the three days is up, including receipts for everything you had to buy in the interim.

Your travel companion lets you down

Whether it's a breakup or a friend cancelling, it sucks and can ramp up costs. The easiest solution to finding a new travel companion is to go to a well-reviewed hostel and find someone you want to travel with. You should spend at least three days getting to know this person before you suggest travelling together. Finding someone in person is always better than finding someone online, because you can get a better idea of whether you will have a smooth journey together. Travel can make or break friendships.

Culture shock

I had one of the strongest culture shocks while spending 6 months in Japan. It was overwhelming how much I had to prepare when I went outside of the door (googling words and sentences what to use, where to go, which station and train line to use, what is this food called in Japanese and how does its look etc.). I was so tired constantly but in the end I just let go and went with my extremely bad Japanese. If you feel culture shocked its because your brain is referencing your surroundings to what you know. Stop comparing, have Google translate downloaded and relax.

Your Car rental insurance is crazy expensive

I always use carrentals.com and book with a credit card. Most credit cards will give you free insurance for the car, so you don't need to pay the extra. Some unsavoury companies will bump the price up when you arrive. Ask to speak to a manager. If this doesn't resolve, it google "consumer ombudsman for NAME OF COUNTRY." and seek an immediate full refund on the balance difference you paid. It is illegal in most countries to alter the price of a rental car when the person arrives to pickup a pre-arranged car.

A note on Car Rental Insurance

Always always always rent a car with a credit card that has rental vehicle coverage built into the card and is automatically applied when you rent a car. Then there's no need to buy additional rental insurance (check with your card on the coverage they protect some exclude collision coverage). Do yourself a favour when you step up to the desk to rent the car tell the agent you're already covered and won't be buying anything today. They work on commission and you'll save time and your patience avoiding the upselling.

You're sick

First off ALWAYS, purchase travel insurance. Including emergency transport up to $500k even to back home, which is usually less than $10 additional. I use https://www.comparethemarket.com/travel-insurance/ to find the best days. If I am sick I normally check into a hotel with room service and ride it out.

Make a Medication Travel Kit

Take travel sized medications with you:

- Antidiarrheal medication (for example, bismuth sub-salicylate, loperamide)

- Medicine for pain or fever (such as acetaminophen, aspirin, or ibuprofen)

- Throat Lozenges

Save yourself from most travel related hassles

- Do not make jokes with immigration and customs staff. A misunderstanding can lead to HUGE fines.

- Book the most direct flight you can find nonstop if possible.

- Carry a US$50 bill for emergency cash. I have entered a country and all ATM and credit card systems were down. US$ can be exchanged nearly anywhere in the world and is useful in extreme situations, but where possible don't exchange, as you will lose money.

- Check, and recheck, required visas and such BEFORE the day of your trip. Some countries, for instance, require a ticket out of the country in order to enter. Others, like the US and Australia, require electronic authorisation in advance.

- Airport security is asinine and inconsistent around the world. Keep this in mind when connecting flights. Always leave at least 2 hours for international connections or international to domestic. In Stansted for example, they force you to buy one of their plastic bags, and remove your liquids from your own plastic bag.... just to make money from you. And this adds to the time it will take to get through security, so lines are long.

- Wiki travel is perfect to use for a lay of the land.

- Expensive luggage rarely lasts longer than cheap luggage, in my experience. Fancy leather bags are toast with air travel.

Food

- When it comes to food, eat in local restaurants, not tourist-geared joints. Any place with the menu in three or more languages is going to be overpriced.

- Take a spork - a knife, spoon and fork all in one.

Water Bottle

Take a water bottle with a filter. We love these ones from Water to Go.

Empty it before airport security and separate the bottle and filter as some airport people will try and claim it has liquids…

Bug Sprays

If you're heading somewhere tropical spray your clothes with Permethrin before you travel. It lasts 40 washes and saves space in your bag. A 'Bite Away' zapper can be used after the bite to totally erase it. It cuts down on the itching and erases the bite from your skin.

Order free mini's

Don't buy those expensive travel sized toiletries, order travel sized freebies online. This gives you the opportunity to try brands you've never used before, and who knows, you might even find your new favourite soap.

Take a waterproof bag

If you're travelling alone you can swim without worrying about your phone, wallet and passport laying on the beach.

You can also use it as a source of entertainment on those ultra budget flights.

Make a private entertainment centre anywhere

Always take an eye-mask, earplugs, a scarf and a kindle reader - so you can sleep and entertain yourself anywhere!

The best Travel Gadgets

The door alarm

If you're nervous and staying in private rooms or airbnbs take a door alarm. For those times when you just don't feel safe, it can help you fall asleep. You can get tiny ones for less than $10 from Amazon: https://www.amazon.com/Travel-door-alarm/s?k=Travel+door+alarm

Smart Blanket

Amazon sells a 6 in 1 heating blanket that is very useful for cold plane or bus trips. Its great if you have poor circulation as it becomes a detachable Foot Warmer: Amazon http://amzn.to/2hTYlOP I paid $49.00.

The coat that becomes a tent

https://www.adiff.com/products/tent-jacket. This is great if you're going to be doing a lot of camping.

Clever Tank Top with Secret Pockets

Keep your valuables safe in this top. Perfect for all climates.
                              on Amazon for $39.90

Optical Camera Lens for Smartphones and Tablets

Leave your bulky camera at home. Turn your device into a high-performance camera. Buy on Amazon for $9.95

Travel-sized Wireless Router with USB Media Storage

Convert any wired network to a wireless network. Buy on Amazon for $17.99.

Buy a Scrubba Bag to wash your clothes on the go

Or a cheaper imitable. You can wash your clothes on the go.

Hacks for Families

Rent an Airbnb apartment so you can cook

Apartments are much better for families, as you have all the amenities you'd have at home. They are normally cheaper per person too. We are the first travel guide publisher to include Airbnb's in our recommendations if you think any of these need updating you can email me at philgtang@gmail.com

Shop at local markets

Eat seasonal products and local products. Get closer to the local market and observe the prices and the offer. What you can find more easily, will be the cheapest.

Take Free Tours

Download free podcast tours of the destination you are visiting. The podcast will tell you where to start, where to go, and what to look for. Often you can find multiple podcast tours of the same place. Listen to all of them if you like, each one will tell you a little something new.

Pack Extra Ear Phones

If you go on a museum tour, they often have audio guides. Instead of having to rent one for each person, take some extra earphones. Most audio tour devices have a place to plug in a second set.

Buy Souvenirs Ahead of Time

If you are buying souvenirs somewhere touristy, you are paying a premium price. By ordering the same exact products online, you can save a lot of money.

Use Cheap Transportation

Do as the locals do, including weekly passes.

Carry Reusable Water Bottles

Spending money on water and other beverages can quickly add up. Instead of paying for drinks, take some refillable water bottles.

Combine Attractions

Many major cities offer ticket bundles where one price gets you into 5 or 6 popular attractions. You will need to plan ahead of time to decide what things you plan to do on vacation and see if they are selling these activities together.

Pack Snacks

Granola bars, apples, baby carrots, bananas, cheese crackers, juice boxes, pretzels, fruit snacks, apple sauce, grapes, and veggie chips.

Stick to Carry-On Bags

Do not pay to check a large bag. Even a small child can pull a carry-on.

Visit free art galleries and museums

Just google the name + free days.

Eat Street Food

There's a lot of unnecessary fear around this. You can watch the food prepared. Go for the stands that have a steady queue.

Travel Gadgets for Families

Dropcam

Are what-if scenarios playing out in your head? Then you need Dropcam.

'Dropcam HD Internet Wi-Fi Video Monitoring Cameras help you watch what you love from anywhere. In less than a minute, you'll have it setup and securely streaming video to you over your home Wi-Fi. Watch what you love while away with Dropcam HD.'

Approximate Price: $139

Kelty-Child-Carrier

Voted as one of the best hiking essentials if you're traveling with kids and can carry a child up to 18kg.

Jetkids Bedbox

No more giving up your own personal space on the plane with this suitcase that becomes a bed.

Safety

"If you think adventure is dangerous, try routine. It's lethal." – Paulo Coelho

Backpacker murdered is a media headline that leads people to think traveling is more dangerous than it is. The media sensationalise the rare murders and deaths of backpackers and travellers. The actual chances of you dying abroad are extremely extremely low.

Let's take the USA as an example. In 2018, 724 Americans **died** from unnatural causes, 167 died from car accidents, while the majority of the other deaths resulted from drownings, suicides, and non-vehicular accidents. Contrast this with the 15,000 murders in the US in 2018, and travelling abroad looks much safer than staying at home.

There are many things you can to keep yourself safe. Here are our tips.

1. Always check fco.co.uk before travelling. NEVER RELY on websites or books. Things are changing constantly and the FCO's (UK's foreign office) advice is always UP TO DATE (hourly) and **extremely conservative.**

2. Check your mindset. I've travelled alone to over 180 countries and the main thing I learnt is if you walk around scared, or anticipating you're going to be pickpocketed, your constant fear will attract bad energy. Murders or attacks on travellers are the mainstay of media, not reality, especially in countries familiar with travellers. The only place I had cause to genuinely fear for my life was Papua New Guinea -

where nothing actually happened to me only my own panic over culture shock.

There are many things you can do to stop yourself being victim to the two main problems when travelling: theft or being scammed.

I will address theft first. Here are my top tips:

- Stay alert while you're out and always have an exit strategy.

- Keep your money in a few different places on your person and your passport somewhere it can't be grabbed.

- Take a photo of your passport on your phone in case. If you do lose it, google for your embassy, you can usually get a temporary pretty fast.

- Google safety tips for travelling in your country to help yourself out and memorise the emergency number.

- At hostels, keep your large bag in the room far under the bed/out of the way with a lock on the zipper.

- On buses/trains, I would even lock my bag to the luggage rack.

- Get a personal keychain alarm. The sound will scare anyone away.

- Don't wear any jewellery. A man attempted to rob a friend of her engagement ring in Bogota, Colombia, and in hindsight I wished I'd told her to leave it at home/wear it on a hidden necklace, as the chaos it created was avoidable.

- Don't turn your back to traffic while you use your phone.

- When travelling in the tuktuk sit in the middle and keep your bag secure. Wear sunglasses as dust can easily get in your eyes.

- Don't let anyone give you flowers, bracelets, or any type of trinket, even if they insist it's for free and compliment you like crazy.

- Don't let strangers know that you are alone - unless they are travel friends ;-)

- Lastly, and most importantly -Trust your gut! If it doesn't feel right, it isn't.

How I got hooked on budget travelling

'We're on holiday' is what my dad used to say to justify getting us in so much debt we lost our home and all our things when I was 11. We moved from the suburban bliss of Hemel Hempstead to a run down council estate in inner-city London, near my dad's new job as a refuge collector, a fancy word for dustbin man. I lost all my school friends while watching my dad go through a nervous breakdown.

My dad loved walking up a hotel lobby desk without a care in the world. So much so, that he booked overpriced holidays on credit cards. A lot of holidays. As it turned out, we couldn't afford any of them. In the end, my dad had no choice but to declare bankruptcy. When my mum realised, he'd racked up so much debt our family unit dissolved. A neat and perhaps as painless a summary of events that lead me to my life's passion: budget travel that doesn't compromise on fun, safety or comfort.

I started travelling full-time at the age of 18. I wrote the first Super Cheap Insider guide for friends visiting Norway - which I did for a month on less than $250. When sales reached 10,000 I decided to form the Super Cheap Insider Guides company. As I know from first-hand experience debt can be a noose around our necks, and saying 'oh come on, we're on vacation' isn't a get out of jail free card. In fact, its the reverse of what travel is supposed to bring you - freedom.

Before I embarked upon writing Super Cheap Insider guides, many, many people told me that my dream was impossible. Travelling on a budget could never be comfortable. I hope this guide has proved to you what I have known for a long-time: budget travel can feel luxurious when you know and use the insider hacks.

And apologies if I depressed you with my tale of woe. My dad is now happily remarried and works as a chef in London at a fancy hotel - the kind he used to take us to!

A final word...

There's a simple system you can use to think about budget travel. In life, we can choose two of the following: cheap, fast, or quality. So if you want it Cheap and fast you will get a lower quality service. Fast-food is the perfect example. The system holds true for purchasing anything while travelling. I always choose cheap and quality, except at times where I am really limited on time. Normally, you can make small tweaks to make this work for you. Ultimately, you must make choices about what's most important to you and heed your heart's desires.

'Your heart is the most powerful muscle in your body. Do what it says.' Jen Sincero

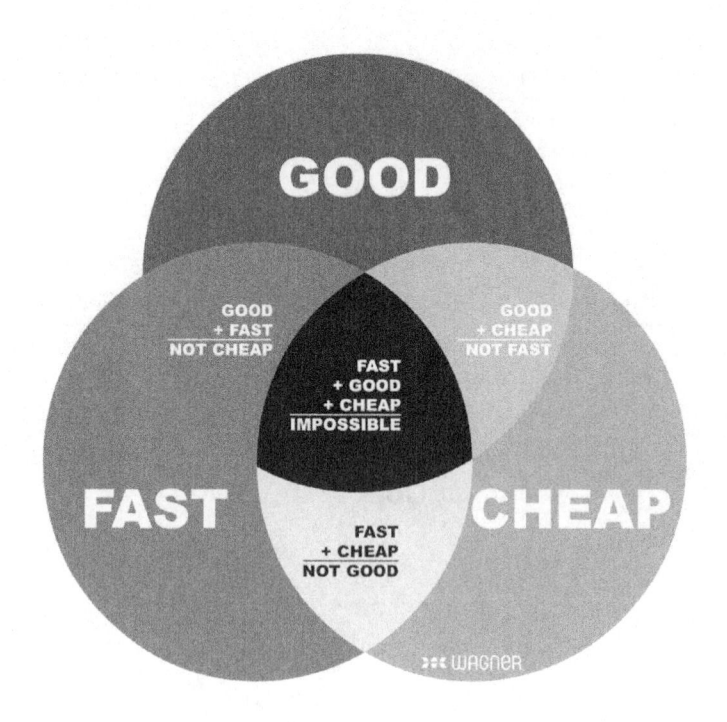

Our Writers

Phil Tang was born in London to Irish immigrant, Phil graduated from The London School of Economics with a degree in Law. Now he travels full-time in search of travel bargains with his wife, dog and a baby and a toddler.

Ali Blythe has been writing about amazing places for 17 years. He loves travel and especially tiny budgets equalling big adventures nearly as much as his family. He recently trekked the Satopanth Glacier trekking through those ways from where no one else would trek. Ali is an adventurer by nature and bargainist by religion.

Michele Whitter writes about languages and travel. What separates her from other travel writers is her will to explain complex topics in a no-nonsense, straightforward way. She doesn't promise the world. But always delivers step-by-step methods you can immediately implement to travel on a budget.

Lizzy McBraith, Lizzy's input on Super Cheap Insider Guides show you how to stretch your money further so you can travel cheaper, smarter, and with more wanderlust. She loves going over land on horses and helps us refine each guide to keep them effective. **If you've found this book useful, please consider leaving a short review on Amazon. it would mean a lot.Copyright**

If you've found this book useful, please select five stars on Amazon, it would mean genuinely make my day to see I've helped you.

Copyright

Published in Great Britain in 2023 by Super Cheap Insider Guides LTD.

Copyright © 2023 Super Cheap Insider Guides LTD.

The right of Phil G A Tang to be identified as the Author of the Work has been asserted in accordance with the Copyright, Designs and Patents Act 1988.

All rights reserved.

No part of this publication may be reproduced, stored in a retrieval system, or transmitted, in any form or by any means without the prior written permission of the publisher, nor be otherwise circulated in any form of binding or cover other than that in which it is published and without a similar condition being imposed on the subsequent purchaser.

All rights reserved. No part of this publication may be reproduced, distributed, or transmitted in any form or by any means, including photocopying, recording, or other electronic or mechanical methods, without the prior written permission of the publisher, except in the case of brief quotations embodied in critical reviews and certain other non-commercial uses permitted by copyright law.

Redefining Super Cheap	11
How to Enjoy ALLOCATING Money in Alaska	24
How to feel RICH in Anchorage	27
Try an all-in-one accommodation	31
Get 50% off an Alaskan Cruise	32
State Park Lands	37
LOCAL INSIGHTS FOR DRIVING	39
More Itinerary Ideas	42
Priceline Hack to get a Luxury Hotel on the Cheap	48
Hotels with frequent last-minute booking discounts in Anchorage	49
Saving money on Alaska Food	54
How to be a green tourist in Alaska	56
How to use this book	60
OUR SUPER CHEAP TIPS…	61
How to Find Super Cheap Flights to Alaska	63
How to Find CHEAP FIRST-CLASS Flights to Alaska	67
More flight tricks and tips	71
How to Find CHEAP FIRST-CLASS Flights to Alaska	72
Visit Reindeer on the cheap	83
Get something for free	87

Explore Juneau	93
Mendenhall Glacier Visitor Center	95
Go Whale Watching	97
Go fishing	99
Visit Valdez	110
Go Gold Panning	111
Bush Mail Flight	113
Sitka National Historical Park	116
Whittier and Prince William Sound	118
Visit the Largest lake in Alaska	120
Breakdown	129
Money Mistakes in Alaska	133
The secret to saving HUGE amounts of money when travelling to Alaska is…	134
MAP of key attractions	137
RV Route MAP	138
Thank you for reading	141
Bonus Travel Hacks	143
Common pitfalls when it comes to allocating money to your desires while traveling	144
Hack your allocations for your Alaska Trip	147
MORE TIPS TO FIND CHEAP FLIGHTS	150
What Credit Card Gives The Best Air Miles?	156
Frequent Flyer Memberships	160

How to get 70% off a Cruise	161
Pack like a Pro	162
Relaxing at the Airport	165
How to spend money	166
How to save money while travelling	171
Travel Apps That'll Make Budget Travel Easier	172
How NOT to be ripped off	174
Small tweaks on the road add up to big differences in your bank balance	180
Where and How to Make Friends	183
When unpleasantries come your way…	184
Hacks for Families	194
Safety	197
How I got hooked on budget travelling	200
A final word…	202
Our Writers	203
Copyright	205

Printed in Great Britain
by Amazon